WEIRD BRITISH COLUMBIA PLACES

**Humorous, Bizarre, Peculiar & Strange
Locations & Attractions across the Province**

WEIRD BRITISH COLUMBIA PLACES

Humorous, Bizarre, Peculiar & Strange
Locations & Attractions across the Province

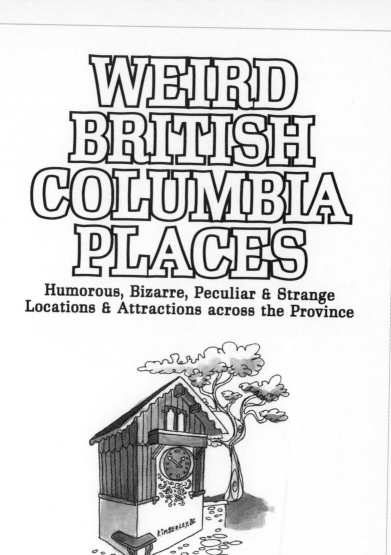

KIMBERLEY.BC

Michelle Simms

BLUE
BIKE
BOOKS

The Publisher: Blue Bike Books

Library and Archives Canada Cataloguing in Publication

Simms, Michelle, 1982-
   Weird British Columbia places : humorous, bizarre, peculiar and strange locations and attractions across the province / Michelle Simms ; Roger Garcia, Graham Johnson, illustrators.

   ISBN-13: 978-1-897278-08-6
   ISBN-10: 1-897278-08-X

   1. British Columbia—Miscellanea. 2. British Columbia—Description and travel—Miscellanea. I. Garcia, Roger, 1976–II. Title.

FC3811.6.S56 2006   971.1   C2006-904135-0

Project Director: Nicholle Carrière
Project Editor: Wendy Pirk
Illustrations: Graham Johnson, Roger Garcia
Cover Image: Roger Garcia

We acknowledge the support of the Alberta Foundation for the Arts for our publishing program.

PC: P5

CONTENTS

INTRODUCTION 7

THE GREAT OUTDOORS. 10

A GHOST, A GHOUL, A HAUNTED PLACE, OH MY! . . . 32

HOUSES, HALLS AND BUILDINGS TO REMEMBER . . . 50

H-2-OH NO 68

A FESTIVAL TO CALL OUR OWN 86

WE ARE WHAT WE EAT 113

ISLAND TIME 126

ON THE ROAD. 138

DEDICATION

The funny thing about writing a book on weird places is that everyone, and I mean everyone, has a story to share. For some, it's the strange festival that's the annual highlight of their hometown; for others, it's the bizarre stuff they've witnessed on family vacations. I dedicate this book to all the weird people living and visiting the strange places in British Columbia.

ACKNOWLEDGEMENTS

The completion of this book relied on the assistance of many individuals and organizations who donated time to answer my many inquiries, emails and telephone calls. Volunteers and administration staff for the festivals and parades that were mentioned made sure to describe the absolute weirdness of their event, especially if I could not be there in person. Thank you to the staff of the Victoria Public Library for finding books, articles and videos. Sorry about all the late fees. Thanks also to the friends, friends-of-friends and colleagues who passed along books, shared photographs and, in general, allowed me a glimpse of their personal weirdness. Finally, I must thank my editor, Wendy Pirk, and my publisher, Nicholle Carriere, at Blue Bike Books, who made the journey through the editing process a painless one.

INTRODUCTION

Weird, to me, incorporates any number of things. It means a restaurant that lists snake on the menu, the legends that come to characterize a region, the festivals and parades that celebrate something—anything—other than jazz or wine.

In short, "weird" can be found anywhere, if one takes the time and care to look for it. In BC, one doesn't have to look far. The province houses lake monsters and forest creatures in the Okanagan, it invents holidays in Williams Lake and it chooses to celebrate "nothing at all" in Coombs. I love British Columbia because the weirdness is embraced rather than thinly disguised.

Of course, in the writing of this book, I couldn't assume that my definition of "weird" would extend to everyone. To each his own weirdness, I suppose. So to make sure I was on the right track, I pulled my trusty *Oxford English Dictionary*—Canadian edition—off the shelf and thumbed through to page 1196:

weird adj. **1.** strange, unusual, bizarre. **2.** suggestive of fate or the supernatural.

I'm quite certain that a light bulb near exploded beside my head at that moment. I rushed down the three stories of my apartment building in Victoria, our province's capital, to peer at the back of my car. This thing needs a wash, I thought. Just kidding—though it probably did need one. I looked at the top of the licence plate and there it was, "Super, Natural British Columbia" in shiny blue letters.

Super, Natural BC. If that's not a sign of provincial weirdness, I don't know what is. It's a cute play on words, yes. But it's also a new way to look at the land and people that surround me. I decided to look at the things I've always taken for granted as "normal." Like a licence plate. To look at the everyday and find the extraordinary, the mystical and the unique tucked behind every bend of the road and mountain peak.

In the early stages of my research, I worried that people would be offended when I told them I planned to include their hometown in a book of weird places. I needn't have been concerned. The general reaction consisted of hearty laughter and agreement, followed by, "and if you think this place is weird, have you been to..." British Columbians are rich in anecdote and generous with their stories.

The places included herein do not represent all that is weird and wonderful about BC. Some places I was certain contained the unusual could not be included because of conflicting information or a lack of information at all. Other places claimed to be "absolutely bizarre" but weren't definitively, for any reason, strange. My one rule for inclusion in this collection consisted of my conviction that to be "weird," a place must have more than just an odd name. Otherwise, I could have just called the book Spuzzum and moved on. Yes, Spuzzum, BC, does exist. Approximately 50 people live in the tiny town, immortalized by the band Six Cylinder, who claimed in a song that "If you ain't been to Spuzzum, you ain't been anywhere."

Throughout the book, you can read about "Big, Gargantuan and Ridiculously Oversized" things in BC. These sections contain statues, streets, trucks, even a cuckoo clock, which are unusual because of their size, whether gigantic, tiny, tall or skinny. If it warrants a double take—it's probably weird.

I hope that no one is offended by their hometown's inclusion in this book. That certainly wasn't my intention. I consider weirdness a positive thing to be celebrated and honoured. The places described in the following pages are by no means *completely* weird; they have grocery stores and gas stations, friendly residents and not-so-friendly residents. I've simply chosen to highlight the strange and downplay the normal because it's much more to fun to research, more fun to write and, I hope, more fun to read.

When I attempted to organize the places into general categories, I encountered some problems. Where to put the Denman Island tree house? Yes, it's on an island, but it's also a strange home. Should the Nanaimo Bathtub Races be considered part of a festival or a "great outdoors" activity? You see the problem. In some cases, weirdness cannot be confined to a single chapter. Please remember that inclusion in one chapter does not limit a town or city to one particular brand of strange.

Go wild, BC.

The Great Outdoors

British Columbia's landscape bears the nickname "Playground of the Pacific."

Wild coastal waters challenge the most adept kayaker, trails through the Rocky Mountains exhaust the fittest of hikers and just about any sport you'd ever want to play has a home in BC—even if your sport of choice is naked bungee jumping or bathtub racing.

If you're short on playmates, legendary creatures such as Sasquatch and the Ogopogo are happy to join in the fun.

That is, if you're lucky enough to spot them.

LOYAL NANAIMO BATHTUB SOCIETY
NANAIMO

With a name like the Loyal Nanaimo Bathtub Society, I would expect the members to be moralistic citizens concerned about the cleanliness and hygiene of Nanaimo's residents. Instead, the society can be held responsible for the growth and development of bathtub racing worldwide. I hope it markets the sport as one where it's mighty difficult for anyone to play dirty!

A bit of history: for Canada's centennial in 1967, the city of Nanaimo wanted to host a special event. That summer, close to 200 tubbers entered the fun event, racing in every kind of bathtublike craft imaginable. The event organizers were shocked when 47 of these not-so-seaworthy crafts completed the 60 kilometre racecourse to Fisherman's Cove in Vancouver, which meant crossing the Strait of Georgia. Two years later, the first sanctioned bathtub race took place in Kelowna, where the chairman of water events was looking to expand the Kelowna Regatta. Spurred on by the success of the Kelowna event, the Loyal Nanaimo Bathtub Society promoted bathtub racing as a sport and encouraged other communities to introduce it to their local summer festivals. The sanctioning committee back in Nanaimo created the World Cup Sanctioned Bathtub Racing Series. Today, tubbers race throughout BC, Alberta and Washington State, as well as in Australia! The Nanaimo race remains the most famous.

Now, the "Great Race" starts and finishes at Departure Bay in Nanaimo, following a loop route around Entrance Island and Winchelsea Island. In the early years of the race, it was a challenge, and a safety risk, just to get past the choppy starting line. Competitors can race in either of two categories, depending on their experience and the class of their vessel. Some boats cost thousands of dollars. Winning tubs usually pull up to shore after about 90 minutes of tubbing the seas. In the evening after the event, fireworks light up the sky as a conclusion to the four-day Marine Festival that celebrates the "spirit of tubbing."

In homage to the event, which started as an addition to the Canadian Centennial festivities in 1967, how about tub racing as a new event for the 2010 Olympics in Vancouver?

CHINA NOSE?

HOUSTON

The story of China Nose Mountain mystifies me. Two theories regarding the history of the mountain's bizarre name exist. Which theory is most accurate is anyone's guess.

China Nose Mountain, located south of Old Man Lake (descriptive names, eh?) straddles the boundary between the Morice and the Lakes Forest Districts.

Both stories date back to the gold panning years, when mining companies and independent panners worked side by side. Mining companies would employ hundreds of immigrant Chinese workers to perform the more dangerous mining tasks—for little compensation—with the justification that they should be glad for the work. Today, most people who own mineral claims in the area dig or pan on the side, or as a hobby, but only mining companies pull out enough to be profitable.

Some say the mountain takes its name because it is shaped like a Chinese man's nose, but from a picture, I can't see it. The mountain juts out from the treed hills around it, with a sharp peak and a sheer face down one side, which drops into a wetland complex. At the top, deep crevasses and sloping ridges dart around each other. Dramatic, yes. But how anyone decided the mountain was shaped like a nose (of any nationality) is beyond my comprehension.

The other, more interesting story about the mountain has never been proven. Some say that a Chinese man who worked for the railway in those years would often disappear into the mountains for weeks at a time and would always return with a bag of gold. Many men attempted to follow him on his profitable journeys, but they always lost the track. When questioned about his travels and the gold's origin, the man would only smile, point to his forehead and say, "China knows."

The weirdest part of all is, what happened to all his gold, and why did he choose to work for the railway with an inexhaustible supply of gold at his disposal? Perhaps it is just a story, but I still prefer it to the other possible origin of the name of China Nose Mountain.

Loaf in Hand

During World War II, citizens of Vancouver worried that the bright advertising signs downtown would attract Japanese bombers. So the lights were turned off, and Neon Products, a local company, had nothing to do until Alf Farmer, one of its employees, had an idea: instead of neon, how about giant, three-dimensional billboards?

The idea sold well, and soon the company was busy again. One of the most notable advertisements from this era was the giant "Loaf and Hand" advertising a bakery. The disembodied hand holding the loaf looked like the Addams Family's Thing on steroids. If only the Loaf in Hand creators had found a way to waft the smell of baking bread over the city—the bakery would have been the busiest in the city.

SASQUATCH PROVINCIAL PARK AND THE HEADLESS VALLEY

The word "sasquatch" derives from the Coast Salish Indian word *sasquac,* meaning "a mythical or natural being that posses a spirit that is better left alone." *Or,* the name "sasquatch" was coined by J.W. Burns, an American schoolteacher living in BC, and is derived from a Chehalis word meaning "wild man." No matter where the name originated, the existence of such a being is rarely debated by British Columbians; over 200 sightings have been recorded in places as diverse as British Columbia itself: the Fraser Valley, Tofino, Creston and the Okanagan Valley. Dr. John Bigdernagel, a Vancouver Island wildlife biologist and British Columbia's foremost expert on the sasquatch, stated: "It is my conviction that the sasquatch, or bigfoot, is real, and that its very existence has generated the myths, aboriginal legends, newspaper reports — and yes, the jokes and hoaxes." Dr. Bindernagel collects observational data about sasquatch sightings. He believes that even though no specimen has ever been found, he will one day join the lucky few who have spotted a sasquatch in the woods of British Columbia.

Sasquatch Provincial Park covers 1220 hectares of deciduous forest and borders four lakes—a perfect hideaway for the reclusive creature.

Sasquatch sightings were reported throughout the 20th century, though the myth dates further into the past. In 1884, Victoria's *Daily Colonist* reported the capture of a sasquatch. The triumphant crew had spotted the creature from a train, chased it up a hill and given it the name "Jacko." No scientific evidence of "Jacko" or the capture remains.

The sasquatch, also known as Bigfoot, is rumoured to be an ape-like mammal over 2 metres tall. It possesses a furry, barrelled chest and leaves footprints as far as 2 metres apart. One would think that Sasquatch Provincial Park would be the prime viewing area for these elusive creatures. The Headless Valley, though, became the sight of the best sasquatch story.

In 1910, two miners were found in the Nahanni Valley with their heads cut off. Technology not being what it is today, police attributed the crimes to the work of a sasquatch, though there was little evidence that the killings hadn't been the work of humans. The valley's name changed to Headless Valley after the incident. Today, it's a popular spot for eco-adventures and river rafting.

The sasquatch has been rendered in both male and female forms on totem poles of many First Nations bands. Some bands avoid the animal; they view it as a sign that one faces an early death.

While sasquatches have been reported in other provinces and in the United States, apparently only the BC sasquatch can swim.

In July 1965, a man named Jack Taylor was fishing when he saw two sasquatches swimming to shore. A swimming sasquatch has also been spotted in Harrison Lake, with the added observation that upon coming ashore, the creature prefers to shake itself dry like a wet dog. The most recent sightings of a swimming sasquatch come from the beaches of Tofino on Vancouver Island. As recently as 2002, locals spotted the creature heading towards Meares Island.

Those lucky enough to spot a sasquatch report that it has dark fur that covers all of its body except its face. The few people who have been close to a sasquatch admit that a strong unpleasant odour comes from the creature. I can't help but wonder if we Canadians just grow a little more hair and are little smellier than we care to admit.

SWIMMING WITH SALMON
CAMPBELL RIVER

Campbell River bills itself as the "Salmon Capital of the World," though on a drive through town it feels more like the "Strip Mall Capital of the World." For a few weeks each summer, this city on the east coast of Vancouver Island really does become a salmon capital, when the salmon who have manoeuvred past whale pods, sea lions, bears, seals and fishing lines come to Campbell River to spawn. All the salmon want to do is mate, and they stop at nothing to complete their task, giving up food and even chunks of their flesh.

They make it all this way, past so many predators, only to have thick, black-neoprene-suited people observe their sacred ritual.

Scientists in wetsuits often take to the waters to conduct fish counts during the annual spawning season, and in 1996, Catherine Temple founded Paradise Found Adventure Tours and offered snorkelling tours with salmon as the main attraction. I've heard of swimming with the dolphins, even swimming with sharks. But swimming with salmon? They're not as playful as intelligent dolphins, nor as adrenaline-pumping as sharks.

Nevertheless, from early July until the end of October, snorkellers dive into the shallow pools to find huge numbers of Coho, steelhead, chum, Chinook and pink salmon. Of course, most of the salmon have turned a murky olive green colour instead of shiny silver. They flap their way upstream as chunks of flesh dangle from their bodies before sloughing off. Farther along in the deep pools, brave divers can spot the elusive, giant Tyees.

Right now, Campbell River is the only site that offers swimming with salmon as a recreational activity separate from the standard diving excursions. Why only in Campbell River? Maybe because the river is so wide, maybe because the water is kept to a steady flow by the dam, maybe because the salmon here spawn in such abundance because of the nearby hatchery.

Or maybe because it's just a weird thing to do.

WRECK BEACH
VANCOUVER

I'm happy to report that British Columbians like to get naked. The province is home to the most nude beaches per capita in Canada, as well as one of the world's most famous ones: Vancouver's Wreck Beach. Even though Wreck Beach, just south of the University of British Columbia Campus, is Canada's only legal nude beach, just remember that it borders other clothing-not-optional beaches; make sure to check signs before baring all or you might end up with a fine! (You probably won't get a ticket, but laughter might be worse.)

The 7.8-kilometre-long beach runs from the Musqeaum Reserve to Spanish Banks West. It's kept private by green forests stretching high up towards sharp cliffs. Eagles, kingfishers, pileated woodpeckers and even the occasional escaped pet parrot watch from the hills. After a trek down too many steps, Wreck Beachers are greeted by a pretty typical Pacific Coast beach. The water looks greyish blue and is far too cold for swimming except on the hottest summer days. Sunbathers outnumber the swimmers, pants down. Where else in the world can you spend a spring morning skiing on fresh powder and the afternoon working on an early-summer buns tan?

During summer, there's no shortage of activities at Wreck Beach. Games of volleyball, bocce ball and Scrabble take place daily, and body painting has become a beach tradition. Painters ask for a small donation to the Wreck Beach Fundraising Committee. At Vendors' Row, jewellery and crafts sell all summer long, and of course there's food and drink aplenty, from Peruvian empanadas to Buffalo Burgers to organic smoothies.

Over half a million visitors bare all at Wreck Beach every year, and on the weekends, it's sometimes hard to find a spot to lay out a towel. For most of the year though, large rocks are more prominent than people. Of course, venturing to Wreck Beach

during the off-season is the best time to find weirdness. I've
heard rumours of a middle-aged man who practises tai chi at
the beach, baring all except for a tattered, red baseball cap.

The best part about Wreck Beach—it's free! (Where would you
keep your money?)

THE MAN WHO FELL FROM HEAVEN
METLAKATLA

Put simply, a petroglyph is an impression, usually a carving or
line drawing, on a rock, made by a prehistoric people. Petroglyphs
can be found on every continent except Antarctica. Because
petroglyphs are carved in rock, most cannot be accurately dated,
according to the Museum of Northern British Columbia in
Prince Rupert; their histories come in the form of oral tradition.
Some archaeologists suspect that as oral histories have been lost,
new stories have taken their place to explain the existence of
petroglyphs. A petroglyph that may be thousands of years old
may have had many different myths used to explain its meaning,
as in the case of the "Man Who Fell From Heaven," an intaglio
carving of a human body at the Tsimshian village site of
Metlakatla. *Metlakatla* translates as "where the wind dies down,"
referring to the Tsimshian community located the on water's
edge of Venn Passage in Prince Rupert Harbour.

Some say that a heartbroken youth carved the figure to prove his
worth to the chief—and the chief's eldest daughter. Other, more
traditional histories claim the image is that of the Raven, cast
down to Earth as the blasphemous by-product of a union
between mortal and spirit creatures. Tsimshian legend says the
petroglyph marks the place where a body fell from the sky.

Archaeologists hope that technology will one day permit us to
date the petroglyphs of the world, putting scientific evidence
behind oral tradition. I can only believe that scientific evidence
will prove less romantic than the stories associated with the Man
Who Fell From Heaven.

BOTTOMS UP!
NANAIMO

Nothing sets a romantic mood quite like naked tandem bungee jumping.

For most Canadians, Valentine's Day means cards and candy, maybe dinner out at a nice restaurant. But for the 250 to 300 romantics that flock to Nanaimo's BungyZone Adrenalin Centre each February, Valentine's Day means being strapped to their sweeties 42 metres above the Nanaimo River, with hundreds of people watching and waiting for them to take the plunge. In the nude.

When Fiona Shaw, a Kiwi, immigrated to Canada, she opened BungyZone, the home of North America's only bridge built specifically for bungee jumpers. Nanaimo, a small city on the east coast of Vancouver Island, has long been a destination for extreme sports enthusiasts. The Canadian government sunk two decommissioned war ships to create artificial reefs which draw thousands of scuba divers, and the forested areas around the city are perfect for mountain bikers. Surely then, naked bungee jumping was a natural progression.

British Columbia can't take credit for hosting the first nude bungee jumps; New Zealanders have been baring it all on a bungee cord since 1988. BungyZone initially held naked jumping one day every April, but it became so popular that the centre had to expand it to a two-day event to accommodate everyone. It was moved to February because... Perhaps it was a way to make the event more of a challenge; the average temperature in Nanaimo on Valentine's Day is around 5°C—a chilly endeavour if you're naked. Jumpers often wait up to three hours for their turn, but BungyZone provides hot tubs, a fully stocked bar and other diversions to pass the time. Jumpers can remain clothed right up until their ankles are attached to the rubber cord. The best part—baring it all means bearing no cost. Naked jumpers ride free.

Other than frugality, what would convince someone to bungee jump naked? My only guess is the chance for closet nudists to bare all in the middle of a Canadian winter. There aren't many opportunities. I haven't yet heard of the Great British Columbian Polar Bear Skinny Dip. Any takers?

BungyZone provides coats for jumpers once they've been lowered into the retrieval raft at the bottom, though the coats don't appear to be much more than bum-skirting rain ponchos. Back at the top, jumpers can relax in the hot tub or have a warming drink at the bar and watch the whole experience again on video.

Currently "Naked Weekend" consists of two events: co-ed jumping and a singles competition. The co-ed jumps are the more popular of the two. That's to be expected, I suppose, because being up on the bridge naked with another person is less intimidating, and let's face it, a lot more fun. Rumour has it that the singles competition used to be dominated by guys who couldn't rustle up a date to jump with them, but in recent years, the number of single female jumpers has increased.

What's also increased is the number of visitors who come to admire the aeronautical design of the human body. In other words, those out for a bit of an ogle.

For all those people who thought they were pushing the extremes of winter sports by taking a polar bear swim, British Columbians (and visitors from around the world) who flock to Nanaimo for naked bungee jumping every February have got you beat.

SILLY BOAT REGATTA
NANAIMO

As if hosting the world's most famous bathtub race wasn't enough, Nanaimo offers a weird boating event for beginners and kids, too. Families and teams start to gather their boat paraphernalia early in the year in preparation for the Annual Silly Boat Regatta. Silly Boat Day occurs in July each year at Swy-A-Lana Lagoon as a fundraiser to pay for programs and purchase equipment for the Nanaimo Child Development Centre. The inaugural Silly Boat Regatta raised $4000 for the centre; the 2005 total was over $60,000. That's a whole lot of silly-boat support.

The silly boats can be composed of any recycled material. They must be able to float while supporting one person. But here's the kicker: they must be assembled on site, in four hours. No motors of any kind may be part of the construction, so if it's not windy on the lagoon on the big day, boaters must construct some kind of recycled paddles.

The post-race party features entertainment, lots of food and prizes for the winners. Along with "First Back" and "Most Pledges" awards, the race also celebrates the "First to Sink."

BIG
GARGANTUAN &
RIDICULOUSLY
OVERSIZED

Truck and Shovel

There's nothing odd about a truck and shovel...not even very much odd about a big truck and shovel. The 6.1-metre-long truck built by GM Electromotive for mining use, which weighs in at a massive 170 kilograms, is just such a truck. With 2500 horsepower, the payload of the truck was over 213 kilograms, or 235 short tonnes. That's a lot of numbers, but even to a non-miner, it's obviously one powerful truck.

The truck and shovel were donated to the community of Logan Lake when the machinery could no longer be of use to Highland Valley Copper. City residents must have been stuck to find a purpose for the huge truck, as the city markets itself as a pristine, natural setting, full of animal life. A huge truck in the middle of town doesn't quite fit the image. The imaginative staff of the Chamber of Commerce determined a novel, and hopefully practical, solution. The stairs on the shovel lead up to the operator's cab, and on the landing, a door led into what was once the engine and winch room. This room now houses an office of the Chamber of Commerce.

CHICKEN DROP
LYTTON, AND WHO KNOWS WHERE ELSE....

The Chicken Drop, or alternately, Chicken Poop Bingo, is one of those things that I've heard about but never actually witnessed. It's one of those events that "a friend of friend" has experienced, involving chickens, poop and winning money. I'm sure that Chicken Poop Bingo is played at family reunions on farms throughout the country, but only in British Columbia does a game played with chicken feces become embraced to the point that it warrants inclusion at a community festival.

The Lytton River Festival celebrates two great rivers, the Thompson and the Fraser Rivers, and their role in Lytton's history. The Interior Salish First Nations people have lived along these magnificent rivers for over 10,000 years and are an integral part of the River Festival. No records suggest that the Interior Salish played Chicken Poop Bingo. The event takes place on the Saturday of the three-day festival, held in early September.

The gist of the game is this: someone releases three hens—one white, one black and one brown—in a large, plywood-lined pen with a numbered grid, just like a bingo card, painted on the plywood. For a fee, usually a twoonie, players purchase a number on the board. That number belongs to them for one round. You must root (and scream and shout) for the chickens to "drop" on your square. If the white hen poops on your number, you win $10; for the black chicken, you get $20; and if the elusive brown chicken graces your number, $30 is yours. What a sight the game must be—moms and dads, kids and grandparents cheering for their number to be pooped on. Wow. I figure this home-brewed good time emerged from the rural farms that settled the Fraser Valley. I haven't had the pleasure of playing the game myself, but the "friend of a friend" account I heard made explicit the tension and excitement surrounding a game. Typically, the chickens become accustomed to the game, so they don't "drop" as soon as they hit the floor—prolonging the anticipation. Sometimes they fall asleep.

Like many great games, the Chicken Drop can be learned in a moment, but it takes a lifetime to master. Playing ordinary bingo with a dabber and sheet of recycled paper will never hold quite the same thrill.

THE TYEE CLUB
CAMPBELL RIVER

Picture the Willows Hotel in Campbell River, late in the evening, sometime in 1924. Three friends sit in the wood-festooned lounge: Dr. J.A Wilborn, Mr. A.N. Wolverton and Mr. Melville Haig, the hotel manager. Above them looms the enormous head of a deer. Maybe they're sipping a drink or two. The topic of conversation, like most nights (and days), turns to fishing, and then to the Tyee.

The Tyee—from the coastal First Nation word meaning "the chief"— are Chinook salmon weighing over 14 kilograms. The fish are known for being elusive, strong-willed and line- and heart-breaking. The Tyee, the three men decide, deserve to be honoured and protected in a manner that preserves their posterity and recognizes the dedicated men and women that capture them. And so the Tyee Club was born. Now, over 80 years later, the club still follows the spirit of that night and the club rules that were recorded in 1925.

At an organizational meeting, it was decided that the angler landing the largest salmon each year would win an annual championship button and be known as the "Tyee Man" until the next summer. The list of angling rules is extensive, covering everything from rod and lure to location and boat regulations. The following rules are worth highlighting:

☛ Fish must be taken from the waters of Discovery Passage, bound by Seymour Narrows on the north end and by a line drawn due west from Cape Mudge on the south end. This area is known as the Tyee pool.

☛ Fish must be taken only while trolling (trailing a baited line behind the boat) from a boat being rowed or paddled. Motors may only be used to travel to and from the Tyee pool.

☛ The reel may be any hand-operated type; electric or spring-wound automatic reels are not allowed.

☛ Any fish that has been mutilated by sharks, seals or other forces that may have affected its fighting ability will be disqualified.

In addition to these rules, the club also inspects the anglers' equipment before setting out, and again before awarding any buttons. The "Tyee Man" for 2005 was Paul Breukers, who landed a 21-kilogram salmon in July. This is nowhere near the record though; Walter Shutts of Oregon landed a 32-kilogram Tyee in 1968.

Today, people around the glove know of Campbell River's Tyee Club. Each August, tourists visit Campbell River to catch one of the coveted fish and become a member of the club. Entrance cannot be bought, shared or passed down in a family; members have to catch a Tyee following the strict rules. Because these rules make catching a Tyee such a challenge, the fish has not felt as drastic a loss in populations as other types of salmon in British Columbia have.

Though rods, lines and boats have changed over the years, and modern technologies have devised new ways to give anglers the upper hand, the Tyee Club believes that a greater achievement comes from catching a Tyee under the set conditions. Experience and skillful angling maintains the essence of the sport.

SHORELINE BOG TRAIL
TOFINO

Leave it to British Columbians to create a nature walk in a region where the ecosystem actually fights off plant growth. The Shorepine Bog Trail stands in stark contrast to the lush vegetation and coastal rainforests found in the immediate area, near Tofino on Vancouver Island.

On the rest of the island, shorepines and cedars grow approximately 30 metres high and are characterized by their straight, upward-stretching trunks. The shorepines at the bog seem confused; their branch reach outwards instead of up, giving them the knobby appearance of bonsai trees on steroids. Has anyone considered renaming this quick walk the "Shortpine Bog Trail," I wonder? A writer for the *Tofino Time* website remarked: "The boardwalk trail takes you around a mossy world where stunted, gnarled trees grow like stalks of broccoli on an otherwise barren landscape."

So what's to blame for these dwarfed trees? Pollution? Global warming? No. Sphagnum moss. It covers the floor of the Shorepine Bog, which is a geological depression. The moss soaks up rainwater and turns it acidic. The water feeds into the soil, starving the trees and plants of nutrients. In addition to the shorepine, other hardy plants also fight for survival in the bog. Two such plants—Labrador tea and evergreen huckleberry— were used by the Nuu-chah-nulth peoples for making jams and beverages.

BIG

GARGANTUAN & RIDICULOUSLY OVERSIZED

World's Largest Cross-Country Skis

Once an important stop on Cariboo Wagon Road, 100 Mile House remains an important part of this region's past and present. Many towns along what is now the Cariboo Highway are referred to by their distance north along the Gold Rush Trail from Lillooet (Mile 0). When Canada went metric, I guess the name "116 Kilometre House" just didn't have as nice a ring to it. Dating back to 1861 and originally known as Bridge Creek, 100 Mile House served primarily as a resting place for people travelling between Kamloops and Fort Alexandria. Today, 100 Mile House still serves as a travellers' destination point, but no one comes here to rest anymore. They come for the skiing.

In winter, the sparsely populated town (1823 year-round residents) spikes with visitors flocking to the self-proclaimed "International Nordic Ski Capital." Funny, I'd have thought that capital would be somewhere Nordic, such as, maybe, Norway. The town offers nearly 200 kilometres of machine-groomed trails and hosts numerous races and winter ski events from the first snowfall until thaw. Many of the trails are lit for night skiing, or skiers can make like "Mr. Cross County" Gunner Rasmussen and ski by moonlight.

To prove how serious 100 Mile House takes its skiing, a giant pair of cross-country skis accessorizes the town's information centre. At 11 metres long, with 9-metre poles to match, these racing skis are the longest in the world.

HARRISON LAKE POKER RUN
HARRISON LAKE

Poor Harrison Lake—always in the shadow of the town's popular tourist activity, the hot springs. In the shadow for all of the year, that is, except for one memorable weekend each summer when the Harrison Lake Poker Run takes over. The poker run is not a race. The object is to collect five playing cards from different points around the lake: Rainbow Falls, Inkman Island, Cogburn Beach, Doctors Bay and Long Island Bay. These cards become a "hand." Whichever team has the best poker hand at the end of the day wins.

The event is run as a fundraiser for the Kent-Harrison Search and Rescue, and it regularly sells out. Nearly 100 boats and hundreds of people compete each year.

At each stop, a full deck of cards is hidden. Each card is sealed in an envelope. Theoretically, there could be identical hands at the end of the day, or even the impossible five-of-a-kind, all aces of spades!

There's no bluffing in this game; cards get posted on the wall for everyone to see.

For more competitive players, the Winter to Spring Run, held on the May long weekend, provides a more competitive game. Players collect nine cards at three stops on the lake. In the following poker game, boaters get to keep their cards private. The game lasts for three rounds, and on each round, players can exchange up to three cards from their private stash. The pocket cards can only come out once, though, so players need to use them wisely.

A Ghost, a Ghoul,
a Haunted Place,
Oh My!

"Real" ghost stories, that is to say, ones that are based on the experiences of real people, have the tendency to leave the reader flat. Questions often go unanswered, or worse, unasked; details are sometimes vague, and stories generally lack any sense of closure. On the other hand, "real" ghost stories affect us because they aren't exaggerated for effect, with a grisly murder that unravels on the final pages.
The real ghost stories haunt us.

British Columbia is blessed with more ghost stories and haunted spots than any other province, with the possible exception of Newfoundland. And as indebted as we are to the gold rush years for much of BC's fame and wealth, we also owe that era gratitude for the stories and ghost towns that survive today. Ghost towns and deserted CRP railway divisions dot the province from north to south, east to west, sea to sky. Of course, ghosts don't limit themselves to ghost towns; that would be far too predictable.

In this chapter, we'll explore the mysterious ghostly sightings and haunted spots that spook British Columbians.

A GHOSTLY HERITAGE
BARKERVILLE

One of BC's first traditional ghost stories dates back to the early gold rush years, when miners, prospectors and young men seeking their fortunes flooded into British Columbia. Barkerville erupted into prominence after William "Billy" Barker discovered "lead" that eventually totalled 37,500 ounces of gold. For years, Barkerville boasted the best sights in the Cariboo region. Food and drink, horse racing and hurdy-gurdy dancing girls were just some of the attractions. The grim-to-glory life of a gold panner, along with the high stakes of the drinking and gambling lifestyle it inspired, led to many ghost stories centred around Barkerville. One such story focuses on Wellington Moses, Barkerville's most famous barber.

Wellington Moses had built up quite a reputation before the events that made him famous, and notorious. Moses had arrived in Victoria during the Fraser River Gold Rush in 1858. He prospered as one of the area's first black barbers, but he longed for more adventure than the growing city had to offer. Despite the security of Victoria, he packed up his belongings and headed east to be closer to the activity in the Cariboo region, where men became legends overnight. Once again, Moses's business fared well, but because of the frigid winter months, when many men left the area, he was forced to head towards the coast. He settled in New Westminster.

Here he met Morgan Blessing, a wealthy Bostonian intent on procuring a fortune independent of his family's money. Until he made that fortune, however, Blessing had no qualms about flashing his wealth around—a good way to make enemies thinly disguised as friends. Blessing became known for the "guardian angel" pin fashioned out of a huge gold nugget, which he wore on his scarf.

When the warm weather returned, Blessing and Moses headed to Barkerville together, despite their differences in class, race and profession. Along the way, an American named James Barry joined their party. One night, in a hotel bar, the angel pin went missing. Barry quickly accused Moses of the crime, and Blessing believed him, even though there was no evidence that Moses had the pin. The bar owner threw Moses out to quell the other bar patrons' chants that Moses should be lynched immediately.

Moses travelled to Barkerville alone, where he set up shop once again. A forgiving man, he searched Barkerville for his former friend in hopes of making amends. Blessing never arrived, though James Barry did, along with a suspicious fortune he refused to talk about.

To Moses' relief, Morgan Blessing walked into the tiny barbershop one afternoon, though his clothes were now ragged and torn, and his beard hadn't been trimmed in weeks. The man didn't speak; he just planted himself in the only chair and waited. Moses heated a towel to soak his friend's weathered face, but when he pressed the towel against Blessing's skin, it immediately soaked through with blood.

Moses jumped back, astonished. He begged Blessing to speak, but the man suddenly faded away to nothing—only the glint of dust in the afternoon sunlight remained where his friend had sat. Moses believed that his friend had returned with a message: I have been murdered. Moses had a strong suspicion about who was to blame for the murder, but he had no proof. Furthermore, if it came down to a "he said, he said" situation, a black man's word would not be given equal weight. At this time, even the cemetery was still reserved for white men only.

Then Barry slipped up. Almost simultaneously, the bullet-ridden body of Morgan Blessing was discovered, and one of James Barry's many girlfriends was spotted wearing the "guardian angel." Chief Justice Matthew Begbie, also known as the "hanging judge," found Barry guilty of murder. He was hanged in the neighbouring town of Richfield.

The "guardian angel" had protected neither man. My only question is, what happened to the blood-soaked towel?

LADY OF THE LINKS
OAK BAY

Victoria's Oak Bay golf course prides itself on being one of Canada's most beautiful courses. The 18 holes lie near the ocean, and at one time, the Oak Bay golf course was a centre for upper-class social activity. Today, the Oak Bay neighbourhood of Victoria maintains this dignified air.

Unlike some ghosts, the Oak Bay phantom has little mystery surrounding her death. Doris Gravlin had been a young, popular nurse with an estranged—or just strange—husband named Victor. He worked as a sports editor for one of Victoria's local daily papers, though I'm sure he hoped that this golf story would never make it into print.

On the evening of September 22, 1936, Doris left her work at the home of Ms. Kathleen Richardson on Beach Drive. She told her employer that she wanted to enjoy the warm autumn evening by taking a walk. She didn't make it back. Five days later, a caddy at the Oak Bay golf course discovered a woman's sweater while hunting for a lost ball. As he searched on, he found much more than a tiny white ball; bending down to pick it up, he spotted the body of Doris Gravlin in some tall grasses. In the subsequent investigation, police revealed that she had been murdered beside the seventh hole, then dragged towards the beach. Who ever said that the number seven was lucky? Doris would have something to say about that. The question I have is why did it take so long for her body to be found—and found by a caddy? Where had the police been looking for the missing woman?

The police turned immediately to Victor Gravlin for questioning but discovered that the man had disappeared from his parents' home the same night Doris had been murdered. In time, Victor's coworkers admitted that Victor and Doris had been contemplating a reconciliation, provided that Victor gave up his drinking habit—the reason Doris had fled the marriage.

The former couple had met at the Oak Bay Beach Hotel that night, and friends offered the information that a walk around the golf course had been a favourite activity of the pair.

Victor never returned to Victoria, and many people assumed he had killed Doris, then taken off. Later, his drowned body was recovered, and the story took on a more tragic tone.

The story of Doris Gravlin's murder could have faded into the realm of sad local stories, if it had not been for one thing: Doris refuses to be forgotten—and she's got a message.

The first person to spot Doris was a single fisherman. She appeared very close to him but said nothing, just stared out towards the sea. The second time she appeared proved to be the first in a succession of very similar stories of Doris sightings. Anthony Gregson and his girlfriend, who were 16 at the time, were walking on the golf course one evening in late spring. Suddenly, the atmosphere went from romantic to eerie—a grey figure appeared in the distance. Though far away, the couple were positive that they had seen a woman wearing a long, faded dress—and she definitely was not human. The figure seemed to float along the ground, then made her way down to the beach and stopped at the water. She remained there, staring out at the sea, until the couple scrambled away.

Local legend claims that Doris appears only at the seventh hole and only to young couples. One would think that her appearances would make the seventh hole a popular spot for high school sweethearts or couples from the nearby university. The catch is that, according to the story, couples who spot Doris, who appears in her wedding dress, will never marry. Much like Doris would wish that she had never married the man who brought her to the seventh hole of the Oak Bay golf course.

BIG
GARGANTUAN & RIDICULOUSLY OVERSIZED

Spirit Viking

Burnaby has an ideal location at the centre of the Lower Mainland communities, between Vancouver, Coquitlam and New Westminster. Before the early pioneers arrived in the 1850s, tall trees and wildlife covered the land. Development progressed slowly and steadily into the 20th century as the economic base changed from logging and agriculture to commercial and industrial endeavours. The city takes its name from Robert Burnaby, a merchant and businessman who explored the area in 1859 and became heavily involved in community affairs all along the West Coast. To be clear, Robert Burnaby was a pioneer and member of the BC Legislature. He was not a Viking.

And yet, the most eye-grabbing monument in the city is a mammoth Viking bust measuring 3.4 metres in height and 4.7 metres across the shoulders.

Built in 1994, the Viking isn't really a community monument. It serves as the mascot of the North Burnaby High School. A plaque on the Viking reads:

"This statue of the Burnaby North Viking symbolizes the spirit of strength and courage in each of us that seeks new challenges and new horizons to make a better world."

Couldn't "Viking" just have been replaced with "Pioneer" for a more historically relevant message? I guess that being the "North Burnaby Pioneers" wouldn't rouse the same levels of school spirit.

Not everyone in the area feels "spirit" for the concrete Viking. Before construction began, every house on the street across from it signed a petition to stop its going up. Graduates of the North Burnaby High School refer to the structure as Satan, and over the years, the poor Viking has been vandalized to have blonde hair, makeup and even a pink bra.

Not all the Viking's costumes are the work of vandals. Each Christmas, he gets into the holiday spirit with a fur-trimmed red hat for the month of December.

THE PHANTOM GROWLER
STEWART

Before World War I, over 10,000 people called Stewart home. Many dreamed of finding gold in the snow-capped mountains that lined the border between British Columbia and Alaska. Few actually struck it rich. A common practice for those prospecting in the area was to cross the border into Hyder, Alaska and visit the Glacier Inn Bar. Men wrote their name on a bill then nailed it to the wall—if they went bust, at least they could come back for a drink to dull their worries. The tradition continues today, with the "wallpaper" valued at over $20,000.

After a short boom, Stewart's population dropped to under a dozen residents before the logging industry induced new people to the area. Today, the population is a meagre 696. But even after the town's drastic population drop, one Stewart legend lives on. Prospectors and trappers who stopped over at Stewart during the 1920s used to tell stories about a phantom that roamed the hills, growling at everyone who invaded its territory. No matter the season or time of day, no one had ever seen the creature that made the noises, which sounded like a long, agonized moan.

The phantom growler was a minor concern until 1923, when trapper Jess Sethington didn't return home after a solo expedition into the Unuk region along the BC-Alaska border. Conditions that far north can be extreme, especially for a man travelling alone. Though Stewart bills itself as Canada's most northern ice-free port, it's still risky to travel the hills alone. Sethington disregarded the advice of locals and ventured into the woods with only his gear, rations and two guns, a .33-calibre rifle and a .38-calibre revolver. A search party went out when Sethington didn't return by his appointed day, but aside from deserted campsites, no trace of the man could be discerned.

The phantom growler stayed placid for a few more years, until the Johnston brothers left Stewart and headed into the forests to prospect the rivers around Unuk River in 1933. Surely the men had heard stories about the old growler, but they trekked into his region and set up camp near Cripple Creek, far from any settlements.

The brothers, Bruce and Jack, prospected for three years without encountering danger, even though more black bears and grizzlies called the area home than people. The men did, however, hear the groans of the phantom growler on many nights. In spite of the ominous sounds, the brothers had put all fears out of their minds. Until one moonlight night when the phantom became very real.

The growls that the brothers had become accustomed to grew louder. When Bruce peered from the men's vulnerable camp, he could see the bushes shaking. Finally, the phantom growler came into view. Bruce charged out of camp with a shotgun and chased after the beast. The growler—for sure a huge grizzly—disappeared into the woods.

After such a dramatic encounter, I would have headed south the next morning at dawn, but the Johnston brothers remained up north through summer. As a precaution, they constructed a small wood cabin as a more secure home base. Good plan, boys.

The not-so-phantom growler attacked again in late August. Bruce was spending a routine day down at the creek when his dog started to bark. Bruce turned just in time to see his dog in a one-on-one confrontation with the beast. Both animals snarled at each other.

The growler stretched out one of its massive paws, knocking the dog into the trees. Bruce fired his gun and was sure he had hit the animal—yet, it kept coming. Bruce fired again into the grizzly's face. The bear dropped to the ground, its chest still raised. Bruce fired his last shot, and finally the beast lay still.

Bruce inspected the gruesome animal, amazed at what he saw: the head alone could hardly be described as a bear's. Suffering massive deformities from five lodged bullets, the head was nearly bare and contained only one eye. The empty socket had grown over, leaving only a deep scar. The skull measured over 30 centimetres long and gaped with holes from missing teeth. After scrutiny in Ketchikan, researchers noted that were two .33-calibre and three .38-calibre bullets—the two types carried by Jess Sethington, nearly a decade earlier.

CRAIGFLOWER SCHOOL
SAANICH

In 1885, the Vancouver Island colonial administration built the Craigflower Schoolhouse to educate the children of its workers and the children of other settlers in the Saanich area. As the oldest surviving school buildings in British Columbia, the school is protected as a heritage site, even though many who have witnessed the ghosts there would love to see it torn down.

Considering the events that came later, the decision to use an old bell recovered from a shipwreck on the rocks off Esquimalt as the school bell seems ominous. The bell from the *Major Tomkins* called students to class from the very beginning.

The school prospered in its early years, as did the western expansion on Vancouver Island, where the majority of resources had not been tapped (or exploited) by the First Nations people in the area. By 1911, the school population had outgrown the building, and new quarters were constructed across the street. The old building served as a home for the school's caretaker, Hugh Palliser. Palliser's accounts of ghost sightings were recorded by the Victoria archives and make up the bulk of "evidence" about the ghost in the old school.

In 1918, a gravel truck sunk into over 3 metres of water after a bridge collapsed. During excavation of the bridge, workers uncovered some small bones. Work continued without much concern—the workers assuming that the bones were the remains of animals in the area—but soon, the men uncovered the unmistakable long, thin bones of a human arm. And then a skull. The bones were sent to the schoolhouse, and soon after, strange things began to happen. Cool winds would blow inside even though the trees outside remained still; the kitchen door opened and closed when no one was near it. Hugh Palliser was known as a practical man who wasn't likely to assume the disturbances were anything other than signs of an old building. But even after multiple repairs, the doors continued to swing, drafts found a way into the house, and lights would flicker, only to be fine the next day. The family must have been terrified to stay in the house with these surely haunted bones nearby, so Palliser decided to dig the remains a new grave, hoping to ease the strange occurrences. Somewhere in the schoolyard (he never revealed where), the bones lie to this day, waiting to be uncovered and work their ghostly magic again.

Like so many other haunted spots in urban areas, commercialism has come to play a part at the Craigflower Schoolhouse. "Haunted" dinner parties were once held in the dining hall, with a hired piper to stroll around the outside playing spooky Gaelic tunes.

CHERRY BANK HOTEL
VICTORIA

The Cherry Bank Hotel in downtown Victoria has always felt otherworldly. Inside, the hallways and tiny staircases twist around each other like an intricate jigsaw puzzle, made all the more confusing because everything has been painted, carpeted or upholstered in a deep red. Only the ceiling and door frames remain white. The colour and all the narrow passages make first-time visitors feel like they've stepped onto the movie set of *The Shining*. Old horse racing pictures dot the walls, but the lighting is kept so dim that you'd have to nearly press your nose up against them to make out any details.

James Graham Brown built the Cherry Bank in 1897 as a home for his family and named it after the orchard edging the building. When their children left home, the Browns were left with a 26-room house. They rented to boarders but soon sold to new owners. By 1933, the Cherry Bank had changed hands many times and finally opened as a hotel in the early 1940s. With all the ownership changes, no one can pinpoint the exact year the hauntings began. Over the years, staff reported doors that refused to stay shut and windows that would slam after they had been locked tight. In 1977, a janitor complained that he couldn't vacuum the floor because some practical joker kept pulling the plug out of the socket whenever the janitor was out of eyesight. All the employees were questioned, but it turned out that no one else had been working that morning.

Many sightings have been reported at the Cherry Bank, including a little boy and a woman in a long dress. Descriptions of these apparitions are vague and are not corroborated. But two ghosts in particular like to make their presence known. A young girl allegedly runs the hallways, inviting people to join her for tea in her room, number four. So many people saw the girl that, in 2004, a paranormal investigation group set up camp in room four for a number of days. The results were inconclusive, but the group said they had picked up "a lot" of activity. The other ghost, an elderly woman, has a long history at the Cherry Bank. She lived at the hotel as a permanent resident for many years and always took her dinner at table 15 in the dining hall, where she enjoyed a glass of sherry and the sparerib dinner most nights. She grew increasingly blind and ill, and by 1975, it was clear that she should be moved to a residence with care facilities. She protested the move and passed away soon after settling into her new home. She returned to the Cherry Bank with a vengeance. In the dining room, servers have found place settings removed from tables or knocked around, usually at table 15.

The Cherry Bank had more than its share of ghostly activity, but most hotels and restaurants in Victoria have experienced some unexplainable behaviour. For this reason, a "Dinner Ghosts" program runs from the middle of October through Halloween each year. Groups can dine at many of the cities' haunted restaurants with guides to share all the grisly details. The Cherry Bank is no longer a stop on the "Dinner Ghosts" program. It closed for good on November 4, 2005.

VALLEY OF THE GHOSTS
SANDON

At one time, the city of Sandon was known as the "Monte Carlo of North America." During the 1890s, the discovery of precious metals brought the first settlers to the Kootenays. Rich copper and silver deposits led to the valley nickname, "Silvery Slocan," with Sandon as its capital. During the valley's boom years, Sandon housed 29 hotels, 28 saloons, three breweries, opera houses and theatres, a cigar factory and one of the largest red-light districts in Western Canada. No wonder so many miners, con men and land speculators packed up and moved to Sandon. Although the silver deposits probably had something to do with it, too.

Some say that the city of Sandon was never meant to be. Twice in its history, fire or flood demolished the downtown area. Only the perseverance of J.M. Harris saved the town each time. He financially backed those who wished to rebuild, and he faithfully rebuilt the downtown core and financed the declining mines. After the second disaster, the population had dwindled to fewer than 100, and few could be persuaded to try their luck in the doomed city again. J.M. Harris died in Sandon, the city that had made him rich, in 1953. He was 89 years old and still clung to the belief that Sandon would make a comeback. Some say that the old man haunts the town that failed him. He roams the hills with the ghosts of lonely miners, and watches over the remaining buildings in the city. It seems that Harris does a better job as protector from beyond the grave: no other major fires, floods or disasters have hit Sandon since his death.

Sandon is the heart of a region known as the "Valley of the Ghosts," which runs from Kaslo to New Denver. The majority of towns that line, or used to line, the valley survive today as abandoned hotels and forgotten mine shafts that once brought life to the region. Sandon is no exception. In its heyday, the city boasted a population of over 5000. Today: 15.

BEBAN HOUSE
NANAIMO

Nanaimo residents may have forgotten the timber baron who built and made famous the Beban House on Bowen Street, but most everyone could tell you something about the little boy who haunts the old house today. Frank Beban had been a superb athlete in his day, but his passion was horse racing. He owned and trained thoroughbreds from his home and soon had to build a trophy room for all his awards. After his death, the house and surrounding yards were used as a sports park, while the house remained empty.

Although the house is barely over a century old, the architecture is unique to Vancouver Island—it was the first house to contain coloured porcelain fixtures in the bathroom. They were pink! After being named a heritage site, the old house became the home of Tourism Nanaimo and a daycare centre opened on the main floor. Soon, children who came to the centre started seeing a child who carried a red ball. The child wore a dress, and its hair was pulled back in a tight braid. The daycare operators dismissed the sightings; many children have imaginary friends. But years went by, and the drawings the children made of the little ghost stayed remarkably similar. Though no adult ever saw the child, Jack Bernard, Tourism Nanaimo's general manager, heard footsteps running up and down the stairs that sounded like a child's light step. In recent years, it has been suggested that the mystery child is the ghost of a child who died in the house years ago, the son of a Chinese servant.

For years, it had been assumed the ghost was female, because of the long nightgown, but researches have suggested that a nightgown and braided hair would have been the accepted dress for a young Chinese boy in the early 20th century. At least he finally has someone to play with.

THE PORTRAIT OF A LADY...OR NOT
FREDRICKSON HOUSE, CHILLIWACK

The Mona Lisa may be the most famous portrait of a lady, with a sneaky grin that sometimes appears as a frown and eyes that seem to follow anyone who looks at her face. But in Chilliwack, one can find a spookier portrait...one that hasn't been finished yet.

Hetty Fredrickson, who lived in the Chilliwack house with her husband and family, believed that one of the upstairs rooms was haunted. Dresser drawers opened and closed of their volition, and the heavy iron bed moved around the room. She began to have a reoccurring nightmare in which she saw the body of a woman lying in the upstairs hallway. With her artist's eye, Mrs. Fredrickson could describe in detail the red and yellow dress and mummified appearance of the lady. Not one to frighten easily, Hetty waited up one night, hoping to see the ghost while she was awake. Three nights later she encountered the woman, who appeared only as a cloudy figure.

Disappointed, Mrs. Fredrickson began to work on a portrait of the ghost. She spent days on the large canvas, but left half of the face unfinished. Like Oscar Wilde's *The Picture of Dorian Gray*, the portrait took on a life of its own. The face gradually became more detailed, especially on the side Hetty had left unfinished. But the painting began to resemble a man. A moustache appeared, and the face hardened with dark shadows.

In an attempt to quash rumours that she was making the stories up, Mrs. Fredrickson invited the public to her home to see for themselves. Her plan worked in part, but such a crowd turned up that she could hardly accommodate everyone who wanted to see the portrait. The house became a tourist attraction, with more than 200 cars pulling up on some days. The family sold the house, donated the haunted picture to the Pacific National Exhibition and moved on.

SLEEPY SPIRIT
VANCOUVER ISLAND

Does a ghostly farmer live on Vancouver Island, still tending to the chickens he once raised? Maybe. Some people believe that Vancouver Island is home to more ghosts than any other area of British Columbia. The Wighton family would certainly agree; the noisy sleeper in the upstairs bedroom on their farm has persisted for decades.

The Wighton family moved to Vancouver Island after World War I and settled in a small farming cabin while they waited for their house to be built. On the first night, the daughter, Margery, and her mother complained of a snoring sound in the upstairs bedroom. The family investigated but could find nothing to account for the noise. Night after night, the snoring persisted. Eventually, Margery moved downstairs to sleep on a couch so she could have a good night's sleep.

Builders completed the new home, which the family gratefully moved into, and they promptly forgot about the nosy snorer in the cabin's upstairs bedroom. Years later, after the family had sold the farm, the new owner put a guest up in the cabin for the night. Before he could fall asleep, the farmer was roused out of bed by pounding on his door. The upset guest claimed that the cabin was haunted—just as he was climbing into bed, he heard someone enter the cabin, climb the stairs and drop into bed. Soon after, the terrified guest could hear snoring.

They say that a farmer's work is never done; I'm sure the snoring ghost would agree.

BIG GARGANTUAN & RIDICULOUSLY OVERSIZED

Rosary

It's unclear when the enormous rosary appeared in the yard of a Metchosin home. The wooden cross, strung with blue beads (also made of wood) was the initial phase of a project to build an inn called the Rosary Inn on the property. For some reason, the owner ended up with a sawmill instead. Maybe that's what he'd been praying for all along. Metchosin is horse country on Vancouver Island; it's home to many fine horse breeders and trainers. The name comes from an English pronunciation of *Smets-Schosen*, or, "place of stinking fish." Local legend maintains that years before the Europeans arrived, a beached orca died on the shore of a local beach and the smell travelled great distances. Everywhere the smell permeated became part of Metchosin. That's lovely.

For a long time, a painted sign stood beside the rosary, claiming that the world was going to end in a fixed number of days. When the world didn't end by the appointed date, the owner left the sign up for a few weeks before quietly putting it away.

A WATCHING EYE
PRINCE GEORGE

This story has yet to be corroborated. For now, it survives as the type of ghost story passed around town and shared with family members and friends that come to visit. This local legend says that a former priest haunts the basement of one of Prince George's local breweries. Not a bad spot to spend eternity, I suppose. The details surrounding the priest in question remain sketchy at best. As the leader of a small Prince George parish, the priest was not well known in town. It is unclear what brutal circumstances led to his death, but early one morning, he was discovered hanging from the high rafters in the church basement. He had taken his own life. To no one's surprise, the church struggled to find a replacement; no priest would move to Prince George to inherit a parish best known for this gruesome event. The church eventually had to close its doors.

The building at 600 Brunswick Street stood empty for many years until the owners of Buffalo Brewing Company purchased it. The brewery remains there today, a popular spot for a pint, lunch or a tour. Guests have been known to feel a creepy presence when entering the building, one that builds as they near the basement. Many claim to feel a pair of eyes watching their every move. Could this feeling be the watchful eye of the resident priest, or does he haunt the brewery out of anger that his former church has been converted to a brewery?

Houses, Halls and Buildings to Remember

Sure, the landscape of British Columbia differs from the rest of Canada, with its sun-filled valleys, picturesque urban centres and mild rainforest coast. But what about the people who call British Columbia home?

British Columbians have a certain reputation: tree-hugging, granola-munching, BC Bud–smoking environmentalists. But that's only a stereotype. We're also castle-building, feng-shui-loving, church-stealing architects. When the residents of BC set out to build something, some surprising structures emerge.

BOSWELL BOTTLE HOUSE
BOSWELL

Some people might say, "If you've seen one bottle house, you've seen them all."

David Brown of Boswell might have disagreed. His bottle house, constructed of approximately 600,000 *embalming fluid* bottles, stands out from the rest. A veritable castle, towers included, Brown's construction gives new meaning to the phrase "taking your work home from the office."

In the early 1950s, David Brown was forced to retire from his job as an undertaker in Red Deer, Alberta. He had developed a sleeping disorder that caused him to nod off at all hours of the day, so doctors recommended that he remove stress from his life. Brown had always dreamed of building his own house, and he now had the time to follow through on that. He packed up a small trailer and headed west, leaving his wife to follow when he found a place to settle. As a memento from work, he took a few of the thick, rectangular bottles of embalming fluid.

Brown reached Kootenay Lake and quickly decided he had travelled far enough. He purchased a grassy piece of property and set to work planning his house. He knew he wanted it to be unique—to stand out from the rest. Back in Alberta, Brown had experimented with wood, cement and glass bottles, but he suddenly realized that the perfect materials had been under his nose all along. He just needed to get more...a lot more.

Brown accepted a position as an embalming fluid salesman, travelling the route between Victoria and Ontario in a pickup truck. He sold the fluid and kept the empties. When he had collected enough, he quit the route and started to build.

Driving up to Brown's bottle house today, headlights reflect off the glass bottle bottoms, making the home glow and flicker before falling dark again. Brown didn't face the bottle bottoms outwards merely for aesthetic effect; all the electrical wiring is wound around the bottle necks, neatly tucked inside the walls.

Once construction was finished and Brown's family had joined him, a curious thing started to happen. Neighbours and tourists in the area took to pulling up the driveway to look at the house—some even dared to get out and wander around the property. Reportedly, a friend told Brown that if he wanted the visitors to stop coming, he should start charging admission. How wrong he was. People were happy to pay the small admission charge to see the house. During the summer months, it became necessary to build a parking lot.

Since Brown's death in 1970, his stepson and daughter-in-law have cared for the property—it's still a highlight for visitors to Kootenay Lake.

RICHMOND CITY HALL
RICHMOND

The first time I heard about feng shui, I was reading a popular women's magazine. The article claimed that rearranging one's house, apartment, bedroom or desk according to feng shui principles would increase harmony and flow in the area. If they believed feng shui could alleviate tension merely by rearranging furniture and plants, than it's no wonder the Richmond government latched on to its design principles when plans began for a new city hall in 1990.

There was no doubt that Richmond's previous city hall, constructed in 1956, had to go. The walls contained asbestos insulation, water pipes frequently broke, causing floods, and the concrete construction left the building vulnerable to earthquakes.

By this time, Richmond's population was nearly one-third Chinese. Mayor Greg Haley-Brandt may have been attempting to incorporate Chinese culture into the public sector, but what percentage of the population really gets much use out of a city hall other than as a place to request permits or pay taxes?

To be fair, feng shui gets trivialized by popular culture. Feng shui has been around for thousands of years and is based on five elements: wood, water, earth, metal and fire. These elements must be kept in balance. Lead architect, Joost Bakker, couldn't be expected to accommodate feng shui principles on his own, so the city hired feng shui master Sherman Tai, of Fortune Tellers and Associates, as a consultant. He was the first feng shui master hired by a city.

Master Tai's recommendations included removing a planned fireplace because it would create friction for those using the building, and the addition of a stone cenotaph (representing earth) for the front of the building to produce a calming effect. The ground pools received rounded corners instead of sharp ones, and concrete ground areas were painted brown to more closely reflect earth tones.

The suggestion that is easily the most recognizable to the population of Richmond is the eight-storey administration tower. Tai believed that the tower should be significantly visible from afar. Designers used sandblasted glass to create interesting light effects. During daylight, the sun's rays make the tower glow, and at night, the tower shines like a lighthouse, thanks to a pendant light.

Apparently the feng shui trend caught on: Tai has been a consultant for 11 buildings in British Columbia, including the Great Canadian Casinos, Aberdeen Shopping Mall, the Bank of Montreal's Richmond office and all North American HSBC buildings.

The speed skating oval for the 2010 Olympic Games hosted by Vancouver will be constructed in Richmond. The oval will incorporate feng shui principles too, including determination of racing times in 2010. Western thought holds much stronger beliefs in individualism—that we are masters of our own destiny—while Eastern thought places more importance on destiny and luck, less on will and inner strength. We'll have to wait until 2010 to see if feng shui can give Canadian skaters an extra push on the ice.

THE STOLEN CHURCH
WINDERMERE

Correct me if I'm wrong, but isn't stealing a sin? And the stealing of a church, that's got to be an even more serious offence. Yet that's what happened in BC, and the stolen church survives to this day as the only church in Windermere.

In the days of massive expansion in western Canada, the CPR or the presence of gold determined which spots became towns and cities. Donald was one of the spots chosen as a CPR division.

Windermere had neither of these benefits. People journeyed there to pan for gold or raise cattle, but the town had little agricultural potential. Today, Donald is not much more than a piece of history. Windermere, on the other hand, flourishes because of that new determiner of town success—outdoor recreational activities, such as skiing, hiking and fishing.

The first sign that Windermere wouldn't fade into a ghost town was the arrival of the Columbia Lumber Company in the early part of the 20th century. Finally, the town began to grow. Rufus Kimpton moved his family to Windermere from Donald in 1899. The CPR had moved the divisional point to Revelstoke, so Donald had little to offer the young family. But after arriving in Windermere, Celina Kimpton pined for St. Peters, the little church she had worshipped at in Donald. Rufus, either as a joke or as an act of old-fashioned romance, stole the church for her, moving it first by wagon to Golden, then by boat to Windermere. In total, the church travelled over 100 kilometres to its new home. He reassembled the church on a slight hill, where it remains to this day.

Today, the church is still in use for services and is especially popular for weddings. The "Stolen Church" is a small affair, with clean white sides and a bright red roof. Three narrow windows line each side, and bed and breakfasts host tourists who come to town to check out the famous attraction.

GEEKIE'S GOATS
COOMBS

The village of Coombs grew out of the guidance of the
Salvation Army at the turn of the 20th century. Under
the Salvation Army's leadership, nearly a quarter of a million
poor English and Welsh immigrated to Canada to start new lives.
Many families settled on the west coast, where life was made
simpler by the year-round mild climate. A handful of these families settled approximately 10 kilometres west of Parksville, in the
village of Coombs. Today, just over 1000 people call Coombs
home, but its most famous residents aren't human. The most visited members of the Coombs community are the goats that live
on the roof of the Coombs Old Country Market.

The goats live on top of the market from April through summer, content to graze on the fresh grass that covers the roof, delighting the guests who pull off the highway for an ice cream cone.

Larry Geekie opened the market in 1973 with the help of his father-in-law, Kris Graaten. The goats arrived soon after, deposited by airlift on top of the single-storey building. Animal lover or brilliant marketer, Geekie made a decision that paid off. Millions of visitors have stopped to snap pictures of the goats, which will hold still long enough for a close up if a carrot gets tossed up on the roof—carrots are for sale inside.

I wonder if the Geekies keep the carrots at the far back corner of the market, like milk in the grocery store, so guests have to traipse though the aisles of imported and local products to find a treat for the goats?

BC BUD TUNNEL
LANGLEY

This tunnel belongs in the "what were they thinking" category. In July 2005, authorities shut down the first known smuggling tunnel under the Canada-U.S. border, before the tunnel could even be used, and arrested the three Surrey men who built it.

Marijuana has long been a cash crop in British Columbia, worth an estimated $6 billion annually. The varieties of potent cannabis grown in BC, all under the generic term, "BC Bud" have become the standard for marijuana; the Kleenex of tissue papers. Nearly 90 percent of the cannabis ends up in the U.S., primarily along the West Coast. This BC Bud sells for $900 to $1200 per kilogram in Vancouver (also known to pot-smokers as Vansterdam because of the lax enforcement of regulations on marijuana use), but if it travels to Bellingham, Washington, the price increases to $1800; in California, $3600; and if it travels all the way to New York City, BC Bud sells for as much as $5000 per kilogram.

So the "why" of the BC Bud tunnel isn't all that weird: huge profits.

But the "how" leaves something to be desired...especially if you're smuggling marijuana.

The tunnel began at a rundown white house in Langley, which fronted Zero Avenue and backed onto a shallow ditch that marked the border to the U.S. An old greenhouse sat empty next to the house. The tunnel was almost one metre wide and 1.5 metres high, with a concrete floor, ventilation and a sophisticated video surveillance system. The tunnel ran approximately 90 metres past the border, to a house in Lynden, Washington.

It's unknown how long it took the men to construct the tunnel, but it was certainly longer than eight months. Why? Because that's how long authorities on both sides of the border watched the houses at the ends of the tunnel before busting its creators. I guess those fancy surveillance cameras were facing the wrong direction. A few months after the bust, authorities filled the elaborate tunnel with a cement-like mixture. The three Surrey residents each received a nine-year prison sentence.

THE TAJ MAHAL
DUNCAN

For the bottle house lover, Boswell's bottle house may represent BC's best, but it is certainly not BC's only. The bottle house that once stood in Duncan, on Vancouver Island, became a tourist attraction that drew crowds from all over the world.

Duncan's claim to fame these days stems from its title as the "Totem Capital of BC" or from the world's largest hockey stick and puck, which decorate the Duncan Community Centre. Still, the city of Duncan, approximately 60 kilometres north of Victoria, will always be known as the home of George Plumb's bottle house.

In 1962, George Plumb, a former carpenter and construction worker, arrived in Duncan from Saskatchewan. He purchased property that had once been owned by the Canadian Pacific Railway. The company had constructed some rough bunkhouses and tool sheds on the property, but instead of tearing them down, Plumb enlarged them. For his own home, though, Plumb wanted something a little more unique. "Something unique" turned out to mean a replica of India's famed Taj Mahal constructed out of 200,000 glass bottles. The bottles came rolling in from all over. Friends and neighbours donated wine and whiskey bottles, pop and juice bottles could be retrieved from town and, somewhere, Plumb got his hands on a number of old Pepto-Bismol bottles.

Soon after he completed the Taj Mahal, visitors began to arrive by the carload. Plumb continued to work on the property with a number of supplemental buildings. He constructed a Leaning Tower of Pisa, a well, and (maybe as an homage) an enormous pop bottle. Around the buildings, animals he sculpted in his studio out of concrete or stone grazed on the tended lawns.

The people from *Ripley's Believe it or Not* paid a visit to Duncan to investigate Plumb's strange home, but the eccentric owner felt he hadn't achieved real fame until he was invited to be a guest on Johnny Carson's *Tonight Show*. Plumb played the harmonica.

After Plumb's death in 1976, his home passed through many hands until it finally opened as a bottle-themed miniature golf course. New bottle buildings lined the property, but they showed hasty construction—most of the labels hadn't even been removed. Without a serious buyer, the Duncan bottle house was eventually expropriated by the city to widen the highway. The Taj Mahal that once drew thousands of visitors now made the property unsaleable.

BIG

GARGANTUAN & RIDICULOUSLY OVERSIZED

World's Largest Hockey Stick...and Puck

People from all over the world travelled to Vancouver for the Expo 86 World Fair. I was marooned at my grandparents' home in Victoria so my mom and dad could enjoy the huge celebration. For the festivities, the government of Canada wanted to commission a structure to commemorate the event. Something monumental. Something truly Canadian. They commissioned the world's largest hockey stick and puck.

After the fair, the artifact was donated to BC, which then held a Canada-wide competition to determine which town or city would display it. The Cowichan Valley, the city of Duncan to be specific, won the honour. The newly formed "World's Largest Hockey Stick Society" raised over $150,000 to cover the costs of moving the structure. The 62.5-metre-long stick (built of Douglas-fir beams and reinforced with steel) was dismantled and the heavy pieces (28 tonnes of wood and steel) were transported to Duncan, north of Victoria on Vancouver Island, and reassembled at the Cowichan Community Centre. Cars can spot the giant red, brown and white hockey stick from the highway; at 40 times life size, it's hard to miss. At night, its edges are lit by hundred of lights.

The funny thing about Duncan "winning" the world's largest hockey stick is that Duncan's not really much of a hockey town: it's been home to the Cowichan Valley Capitals, a Junior A team, for 13 years—less time than the giant hockey stick's been in town. In fact, Duncan bills itself as the "City of Totems" because of the many tours it offers of the city's 80 totem poles.

FOR THE LOVE OF JUNK
OLIVER

The South Okanagan is a fertile ground for breeding odd characters. The dry climate is countered by an abundance of lakes, and generations-old family fruit markets stand proudly next to modern wineries. Oliver, in the Okanagan Valley, just 25 kilometres north of the Canada-U.S. border, is known as the "Wine Capital of Canada," a reference to the number of vineyards and wineries that line the highway on both ends of town.

The home of the late Gottfried Gabriel in Oliver is the kind of place the locals know but don't consider weird because it's always been there—like the Dairy Queen. And Gabriel was the kind of man that never let anything go to waste. People driving past the property during the years he lived there did a double take, though, because his property appeared to be a shrine to junkyards of the world.

The property housed collections of hubcaps, flat tires, carnival flags, bikes and plastic flowers, all shaped into massive statues with plenty of chicken wire. To decorate the monuments, and give them a little *je ne sais quoi*, Gabriel accessorized the tops with old saxophones and trumpets or colourful bottles. High up in a tree, a giant Santa Claus watched over the property. A miniature railway weaved through the dusty yard, over hills and under crushed glass tunnels. The work must have taken years of concentrated, organized eccentricity.

After Gabriel's death in 1983, his son fought to have at least part of the property and monuments preserved, but he was unsuccessful. Without Gabriel around to supplement Santa's supervision, vandalism became frequent and the house and monuments fell into disrepair. Homeowners and businesses considered the place an eyesore and weren't sorry to see the shrines go when the property sold and a modern, tidy house went up in their place.

OUTA-THE-WOODS TREE HOUSE
DENMAN ISLAND

Yes, British Columbia goes by the moniker "Playground of the Pacific." Maybe that explains the penchant some BC-ers have towards tree houses. Not just kids, but adults, too. The tree houses I remember as a kid were rough plywood shacks (the better ones had a rope ladder extending to ground). But no one would dare call *these* fanciful homes rustic.

Denman Island can be found smack in the middle of the Georgia Strait, approximately two and a half hours north of Victoria, plus a short ferry ride. The narrow island, only 5 kilometres across, is characterized by sandy beaches, rocky coves and rich forests. Most people who call Denman home are outdoor enthusiasts or artists who make use of the peaceful environment. One resident on Denman Island lives in a spherical tree house, suspended in the air by ropes. Tom Chudleigh's house spans the branches of three cedars, and a spiral staircase wraps around the trunk of the central tree, like a castle tower. At the top of the stairway, a suspension bridge leads to the main area of the tree house, where Tom Chudleigh lives with his chirping neighbours. The house consists of yellow cedar strips with a clear fibreglass finish.

For those who harbour dreams of living in a tree house like the Swiss Family Robinson, (minus the pirates), but can't fathom staying up in the trees year-round, add Wardner to your vacation list. Wardner is located in the Kootenay Valley, surrounded by the snow-capped peaks of the Rocky Mountains. In the middle of a private nature reserve, Outa-the-Woods tree house is one of the few vacation spots that can honestly claim it's unique. The tree house perches 5 metres above the forest floor and rests on seven trees. From the deck, guests can view the reserve's two creeks and private lake, and plan hikes through the reserve's 129.5 hectares of land. Guests at Outa-the-Woods wake up to birds chirping and squirrels running through the spruce trees just outside the window.

SAM KEE BUILDING
VANCOUVER

At the start of the 20th century, in 1903 to be exact, the Sam Kee Company purchased a standard-sized lot at the corner of Pender and Carral streets to build more offices. The company, owned by Mr. Chang Toy, was one of the wealthiest firms in the Chinatown area of Vancouver at the time. Building went ahead as expected, but in 1912, the city of Vancouver expropriated 7.4 metres off the front of the lot—all but a tiny sliver—to widen Pender Street. Mr. Toy was left with a tiny piece of land, 2 metres deep. The city paid Mr. Toy no compensation for the land and further insulted him by refusing to purchase the useless piece that remained.

Everyone expected Chang Toy to give up his tiny chunk of land and move on to a new business project somewhere else in the expanding city. His neighbour certainly thought so; he hoped Toy would move on so he could buy up the land and expand his stores at minimal cost.

It may have been anger at the city or pride that kept Toy from leaving. Rumours persisted that he had stayed on a bet. But I bet it was spite. Spite for a city that would rob him of all but the space it couldn't use, and spite for a neighbour who would profit from his loss. Whatever his reasons were, Toy employed architects Brown and Gillam to design a building for him. The narrow, steel-framed structure they designed was only 1.5 metres deep, but at one time, 13 businesses prospered there. Huge bay windows helped maximize what space there was, as did the extension of the basement well out under the sidewalk—the last remaining glass sidewalk in Vancouver. The building at 8 Pender Street was the only place in Chinatown where residents could enjoy hot baths. Offices and shops took up the main, street-level floor, and the upper level became living quarters. A tunnel was constructed under the building that was used an escape route when opium dens on the nearby Shanghai Alley were raided by police.

Ripley's Believe It or Not recognizes the Sam Kee Building as the "World's Thinnest Building," and the building also holds the Guinness World Record for "smallest commercial building in the world." The building now houses Jack Chow insurance; it still fights with the city about overhang limits.

The newest controversy surrounding the building is that the "Skinny Building" in Pittsburgh wants to steal the Sam Kee Building's records. Pat Clark of Pittsburgh, a "downtown architectural groupie," according to reporter Tim Schooley, appears to be pretty revved up about taking the title. "I'm completely hepped to get in touch with the Guinness Beer folks (the same family also publishes the *Guinness World Records* book) to get their tape measure out to put us inch to inch, centimetre to centimetre against the Sam Kee folks in BC," said Mr. Clark to the *Pittsburgh Business Times*. "If we kick Sam Kee's skinny ass, then baby, we're it."

I'm not sure anyone in Vancouver really cares about all this fuss—but maybe if Mr. Clark gets excited enough about it, the folks at the Sam Kee building will respond in some happily spiteful way. It wouldn't be the first time!

RUN ASHORE
ESQUIMALT

"Ahoy Mateys!" would make a fitting welcome-mat slogan for John Keziere's home in Esquimalt, BC.

Esquimalt, a municipality of 16,500, lies on the immediate west side of downtown Victoria. The name translates as "land of the shoaling waters," and water plays an enormous part in the lives of Esquimalt residents. The community was established as the western headquarters of the Royal Navy in 1865. The original base has been expanded into the Canadian Forces Base, the community's largest employer. But it's not just sailors who live and breathe the sea in Esquimalt.

Down by the marina, a white stucco house tapers into a narrow peak. At the top, something colourful catches the eye, but it's not a flag or windsock. Get closer and you'll realize that it's a pirate, staring out to sea though a telescope. The rest of the house serves as his ship, complete with sculptured seagulls on the roof and an authentic steering wheel fixed on the front, to the right of the door. Thick ropes hang in artful swoops across the upper storey.

John Keziere bought his house in 1980, and he remembered it in an interview with Jim Christy as the ugliest house in Esquimalt. He's been working on the narrow building ever since, when he's not serving as wharfinger on the government dock. I bet he won't be satisfied until she looks ready to set sail. Keziere spent most of his working life on the sea as a sailor and on whaling ships, which allowed him to salvage many of the ornaments that now decorate his home. What he can't salvage, he builds in the workshop behind the house.

My favourite feature? The forlorn mermaid statue in the front yard, flanked by dolphins leaping over the flowerbed. Maybe the beauty is a rendition of the mysterious Mermaid of Active Pass, who has been spotted by ferry passengers, and a sailor or two, on the journey between Victoria and Vancouver.

H-2-Oh No

Water plays an important role in the lives of British Columbians. Bordering the Pacific Ocean, the BC coastline spans more than 27,000 kilometres, and the province's capital (Victoria) and largest city (Vancouver) look out over the expansive waters. Tourists venture here for world famous kayak tours and scuba diving. Treasure hides under murky lakes. Did you know that Environment Canada reported that Prince Rupert is Canada's rainiest and wettest (counting rain and snow) city? And what about the two lake monsters who call BC waters home? Read on for more weird and wet BC destinations.

THE BATHTUBS OF EMERALD LAKE
EMERALD LAKE

Yesterday's travellers were adventurers in search of the extraordinary. They came by rail and horse-drawn coach to a summer retreat on the shores of exquisite Emerald Lake. Legendary guide Tom Wilson first discovered Emerald Lake in 1882 during the construction of the Canadian Pacific Railway. The CPR built the original guest lodge in 1902. By the mid-1920s, the lodge had been expanded, and road improvements made it possible to reach the resort by car. The lake itself gleams like a gemstone because of glacial runoff. As the glacial ice melts, small particles of powdered rock, called rock flour, dissolve in the water, making it murky but still beautiful.

Beyond aesthetics, the murky waters at Emerald Lake have served another, more dubious, purpose. Operators at the hotel in the 1800s dumped garbage in the water, confident that it would not be visible to guests. Another plus to dumping in the water was that bears wouldn't be attracted by the smell.

Rumours of three brass bathtubs submerged in the lake have persisted for decades, though divers have never found them. Bruce Ricketts, one of these divers, reported a conversation held with a man living near Emerald Lake in the 1980s: "...since the lake was so murky, garbage would not have been seen by the genteel patrons of the hotel. It made sense, therefore, that when the hotel was to be shutdown, all the non-reclaimable furnishings, including three bathtubs made of brass, were taken out on the lake during the winter months where they sank into the lake as the ice melted."

Since the hotel expansion in the 1920s, the Canadian government has permitted no additional development. Maybe it figures that developers have done enough damage to Emerald Lake already. Now the area remains one of Canada's most outstanding year-round-accessible wilderness settings. The historic lodge remains the heart of the resort, which is located in Yoho National Park, just 42 kilometres west of Lake Louise.

OGOPOGO
OKANAGAN LAKE

When I was a kid in the Okanagan, the resident lake monster, Ogopogo, was the local legend that set the place I called home apart. Sure, other regions had warm lakes and fruit trees, but nowhere else had an Ogopogo. Never mind that maybe I wondered, somewhere in a suppressed part of my mind, if the evidence supporting Ogopogo's existence was a bit shaky—usually the excited words of a few tourists each summer.

Okanagan legend says that Ogopogo is the transformed shape of a demon-possessed man who had murdered another local, Old Kan-He-Kan, after whom Lake Okanagan derives its name. In punishment for his crime, the gods banished the murderer to the water in the form of a lake serpent, so he would be forced to live at the scene of his crime forever. The creature lived in the caves below Squally Point, near Peachland.

For a time, locals feared the creature would surface and carry away chickens and wildlife. There are no records of this ever happening, but sometimes a brave boater would troll down to Squally Point and offer animal sacrifices willingly. That the dead animals didn't come up was seen as proof that Ogopogo was lurking somewhere below. I wonder if anyone questioned that logic at the time. Tension ran so high that Okanagan residents in the 1920s armed themselves along the shore near Mission Creek, and the BC government announced it would arm an Okanagan ferry against an "Ogopogo Tribe."

The BC government must have been concerned about an attack from a group of warring Okanagan locals, not a green, horse-headed serpent that had never actually been photographed or spotted at close range. At least I hope so.

The origin of the name "Ogopogo" is as arbitrary and random as the sightings of the creature. The story goes like this.

In *Ogopogo: The Okanagan Mystery* (1977), Mary Moon credits Bill Brimblecomb, a guest at a Vernon Rotary Club luncheon, with the naming of the lake monster on August 23, 1926. Brimblecomb sang a song about Ogopogo, the Zulu Chief from a British Music Hall show that was popular at the time. Visiting delegates from the Vancouver Board of Trade enjoyed the song so much that they suggested Ogopogo as a name for the Okanagan lake monster they had heard so much about. The name stuck, and soon a parodied version of the song by H.F. Beattie surfaced.

I'm looking for the Ogopogo
The bunny-hugging Ogopogo
His mother was a mutton and his father was a whale
I'm going to put a little bit of salt on his tail
I'm looking for the Ogopogo
As told me by Harwood (Joe)
The Lieutenant-Governor, the Lieutenant-Governor
The Lieutenant-Governor wants
To put him in the BC show.

In the course of one afternoon, the Ogopogo went from murderous lake monster to bunny-hugging carnival attraction. Today, Ogopogo's fame lives on in the books and stuffed critters in his likeness sold along Highway 97, which runs through the Okanagan Valley.

The Big Seat

There must be a whole lot of very large people in Langley, a city in the Fraser Valley, about an hour's drive southeast of Vancouver. What else could explain the red, 7.3 metre-tall, 2-tonne chair that is located in downtown Langley and was constructed out of solid Douglas-fir? I suppose it could be to draw customers to Valley Direct Furniture, the store directly behind the chair. Maybe. I choose to hope that somewhere in the outskirts of Langley, amid the farms and horse pastures, giants lurk behind every hill and around every corner.

GRAVEYARD OF THE PACIFIC
VANCOUVER ISLAND

With all the resident ghosts of BC's capital city, you'd think Victoria would earn the nickname "Graveyard of the Pacific"— especially considering the city's unofficial motto reads, "for the newly wed and the nearly dead."

Encompassing the shores off Vancouver Island's west coast, the Graveyard of the Pacific has a deadly track record. Over 200 ships have been its victim. It's said that there has been a life lost for every mile of coast. With dangerous, rocky passages, ferocious winds and deceptive amounts of fog, that number is probably a low estimate, because it doesn't take into account the hundreds of small vessels lost in the dark waters.

Like any adventurous pursuit, life at sea gives us heroes, villains and cowards. Early ships, such as the *Boston, Tonquin* and *Lord Western* date back to the exploration years. American vessels like the USS *Suwanee* and USS *Saranac* are proof that no matter how carefully planned the voyage or sound the boat, nature still trumps all.

Of the large ships that sank off Vancouver Island's west coast, three stories in particular remain shrouded in mystery. One, the *Ericson,* was known as an engineering wonder, yet she was overcome off Entrance Island and couldn't outrun the hurricane that finally dragged her ashore.

On December 1, 1902, the HMS *Condor* went missing in a terrible winter storm. Neither the storm nor the wreck was unusual, but as the days passed, the owners knew that the ship's supply of coal had surely run out. Still, nothing surfaced. After a year of searching, no members of the crew had been found, and not a trace of the ship had washed up.

Leave it to a dinghy to survive the wreck! The battered dinghy turned up near the Ahousat village, but it was empty.

Commander Tozier of the United States Coastguard was forced
to surrender his dress sword to the Ahousat chief in exchange for
the small clue. Soon, a life ring, broom and sailor's cap, all
marked HMS *Condor* appeared. The *Condor* officially became
"missing" on March 17, 1902.

The strangest tale attributed to the Graveyard of the Pacific con-
cerns the *Valencia* ghost ship. The SS *Valencia* departed San
Francisco on January 20, 1906, with 108 passengers and 65 crew
members. Only two days into the journey north, thick fog set in
and wind tossed the ship around like a toy. The fierce conditions
forced the *Valencia* into the jagged rocks of Pachena Point,
12 kilometres south of Bamfield. The poorly trained staff was ill
prepared to aid the passengers on the sinking ship, and reports
suggest that many passengers were flung from the lifeboats before
the boats hit the water.

Cue the Celine Dion.

A few strong swimmers made it to shore, where the helpless life-
boat passengers hoped for a line of rope—or anything—to pull
them ashore. The men on the shore disappeared from the beach
and hiked for hours to safety. The shivering men, women and
children in the lifeboats, who had cheated death once already,
died in the frigid winter conditions. All in all, 117 people died
that night.

But perhaps they live on. Lighthouse watchers farther north
along the coast reported seeing the *Valencia* that night, though
there was no way the ship had travelled so far. Years later, sailors
claimed to see a ship that "resembled the ill-fated *Valencia*,"
and they "could vaguely see human forms clinging to her mast and
rigging." The dark night that the *Valencia* went down marked
the beginning, not the end, of the ship's most famous voyages.
Some say that the doomed vessel continues to sail the waters off
Vancouver Island.

JUST *FIND* IT
QUEEN CHARLOTTE ISLANDS

Combing the beaches of BC's west coast has always been a popular activity for tourists and locals alike. The Queen Charlotte Islands, or Haidi Gwai, are hot spots for treasure hunters. A day's normal fare can consist of Japanese glass floats (popular collector's items that were once used by fishermen to keep their nets afloat), discarded plastic bottles and the occasional blanket of dry white flakes that make the shores look like a jellyfish graveyard. While bottles and jellyfish appeal to a select group, crowds of people turned out to comb the beaches in 1990. In May of that year, the *Hansa Carrier* from Japan encountered a severe storm and lost some of its cargo that was bound for the U.S. The lost cargo included 80,000 Nike shoes. The winter following the storm, hundreds of child-size and adult running shoes and hiking boots washed up on the Queen Charlotte Islands. The shoes had spent months rafting the freezing waters of the Pacific, but after a good wash, were fit to be worn—as long as you could find two in the same size. Other shoes (though not in such abundance) were found along the west coast of the U.S. and Hawaii.

BIG

GARGANTUAN & RIDICULOUSLY OVERSIZED

Terex Titan

I remember travelling along Highway 3 as a child, heading from towards the camping mecca known as Banff. Along the way, coming up on the horizon, was the biggest truck I'd ever seen. It towered over the highway, gleaming in the sunlight—a green Titan of a truck—and it was coming straight at us!

Okay, maybe the truck wasn't coming straight at us. It wasn't even moving. But the biggest truck part is no exaggeration, even today, though many a year has passed. Terex Titan is the world's largest tandem-axle dump truck and a legacy of Sparwood, BC's mining history.

The Titan came to Sparwood in 1978 to work the town's coal mines. It arrived by train, on eight flatbed railway cars. The Titan stretches over 20 metres long and nearly 7 metres high; standing beside it, one feels that instead of playing with a Tinker-Toy truck, the truck is playing with a Tinker-Toy you. The only thing that could dwarf this truck is the surrounding Rocky Mountains.

GARGANTUAN & RIDICULOUSLY OVERSIZED During its years in the mines, the Titan could tote up to 350 tonnes of coal per load. To me, that's just a big pile of dirty black stuff. To put things in perspective, picture a dump truck that can carry two Greyhound buses plus two pickup trucks at the same time.

When the amounts of coal being mined dropped off, and fuel costs began to rise, Elk Valley Coal had to retire the no longer cost-effective truck. In 1994, the company donated the Titan to the Sparwood Chamber of Commerce, and in Sparwood it remains.

RIPPLE ROCK
SEYMOUR NARROWS

Ripple Rock classifies as weird not because of anything strange about the rock itself: it was big and kind of grey and really hard—pretty much your standard rock. But Ripple Rock claimed over 120 vessels and 114 lives and was the cause of many petitions before it was finally removed from the waters between Campbell River and Quadra Island.

Back in the 1940s, the dream of completing the Great Pacific Eastern Rail was on the minds of many. Ripple Rock was to be a bridge pier on the link over Seymour Narrows that would connect the mainland with Vancouver Island. Thankfully, the government decided that public safety outweighed the need for an Island-Mainland link. The decision to remove Ripple Rock first went into action in 1943.

The name "*Ripple* Rock" seems to be an understatement. Tides rushed through the Narrows at 15 knots, creating whirlpools measuring almost 10 metres in diameter. These enormous whirlpools, combined with cross currents and vertical currents, could capsize vessels or push them into Ripple Rock like a toy boat in a six-year-old's bathtub. Maybe Poisedon planned to use Ripple Rock as another feat to deter Odysseus from reaching home—but his placement was a bit off. And just like Odysseus, Ripple Rock wasn't going down without a fight.

Attempt Number 1: 1943
City planners first attempted to build a floating platform and drill into the rock instead of tunnelling up and under into the pinnacle, which would have been more expensive. The barge was positioned over the rock with 1100 tonnes of concrete anchors and steel cables. Not such a good plan: the waters became so violent that a steel cable snapped every two days. At the outset, the crew expected to complete their task in three months. By the end of those months,

only 11 holes had been drilled. Drilling under would have been more expensive, but it might have worked.

Attempt Number 2: 1945

Why no one worked on Ripple Rock for two years remains a mystery. It couldn't have been that planners didn't want to risk the same types of mistakes, because the second attempt fared little better than the first. This time the barge was raised over the rock with overhead cables from wooden spars on Vancouver Island and Maud Island. Nine men died when their boat capsized trying to cross the Narrows to get to Maud Island to construct the spars. Work continued through that summer with 139 holes being drilled and only 93 being blasted. Turbulence again hindered progress, and the operation was terminated.

Attempt Number 3: 1958

Boaters on Seymour Narrows were finally safe from Ripple Rock in 1958. After two and a half years of tunnelling from Maud Island into the peaks, the rock was blasted out of the water. Wait a minute...tunnelling? Could that be the same "up and under" plan that was too expensive in 1943? You bet. Dolmage and Mason Consulting Engineers planned the entire project, using three shifts worth of hardrock miners and 1400 tonnes of Nitramex 2H explosives. For those of us scratching our heads at all those terms: the blasting of Ripple Rock was the world's largest non-atomic blast at that time.

Fifteen years after the first attempt, Ripple Rock was finally beaten. Its two peaks now stand at 14 and 21 metres below the water's surface.

THE SPA THAT WASN'T
SPOTTED LAKE

Legend has it that the waters of Spotted Lake possess healing properties. The most famous of these legends recalls a battle between warring tribes in the Okanagan; a truce was called to allow both tribes time to bathe their wounded in the mineral waters of Kliluk, the "lake of wellness." The lake, a naturally occurring phenomenon covering just over 15 hectares, can be spotted from Highway 3, 9 kilometres west of Osoyoos.

The lake contains one of the world's highest concentrations of minerals, including magnesium sulfates (Epsom salts), calcium, sodium sulfates and trace amounts of silver and titanium. To the naked eye, however, it is the combination of these minerals with the long Okanagan summer that makes Spotted Lake so astonishing: as summer passes and the lake begins to evaporate, minerals in the lake's white mud form circular pools across the surface. These shallow pools range in colour from white and pale yellow to vivid green and blue, depending on that year's mineral composition.

Though it is considered a sacred site by Natives of the Okanagan Valley, up until 2001, the property was privately owned—and surrounded by controversy. The owners sought to exploit the lake's rich minerals, while the Native bands opposed these commercial endeavours. The minerals were first harvested during WWI, but not for the reasons you might expect. Chinese labourers skimmed the "healing" salts from the water's surface, which were then shipped to munitions factories in the eastern U.S. Up to one tonne of salts was removed every day.

Ernest Smith, who owned the property, tried to have it rezoned in 1979 to construct a lucrative spa facility next to the lake. Okanagan elders opposed the building, which eventually led to the involvement of then–minister of municipal affairs, Bill

Vander Zalm and John Monroe, the federal Minister of Indian Affairs. All negotiations were stalled after repeated offers to purchase the property were refused.

Nothing much happened at Spotted Lake over the next two decades. But in late 2000, the family of Mr. Smith succeeded in having the development ban lifted. It is believed that bids were already in place to mine at least 10,000 tonnes of mud from the lake (apparently to be shipped to spas in California). Tensions rose again between the Okanagan Nation Alliance and the Smith family. In late October 2001, a deal was finally reached: the federal government and the Okanagan Nation Alliance purchased the property for $720,000.

Today, Spotted Lake remains uncommercialized—an interesting site off of Highway 3. The only sign of its near exploitation is the ragged, wooden building on the property advertising in chipped paint: "Information—Gifts—Souvenirs."

BIG
GARGANTUAN &
RIDICULOUSLY
OVERSIZED

Jerry the Moose

Wells Gray Provincial Park in Clearwater spans 5000 km² of woods and rock in southeastern British Columbia. Home to over 250 of Canada's most spectacular waterfalls, and some ancient volcanoes to boot, Wells Gray is an adventurer's playground. One of Wells Gray's famous animals is the moose. The wildfires that ripped through the area in the 1930s created an ideal home for the animals; in winter, cross-country skiers often have to dodge them on the paths. Though moose are often dangerous, one tame bull named Jerry assisted researches study his species' behaviour. The park adopted Jerry the Moose as its official mascot, and a huge sculpture of him marks the Wells Gray information centre in Clearwater.

CADBORO BAY
VICTORIA

The security and beauty of Cadboro Bay is well known. Victoria's most prestigious neighbourhood, the Uplands, looks over it towards the Juan de Fuca Strait, Mount Baker and the Olympic Mountains. The multimillion-dollar houses in this neighbourhood are built to impress, with sweeping gardens and imposing early-20th-century Faux Tudor—style architecture. Soon after these mansions were constructed, residents on waterfront property received a nasty surprise: a sea monster lived next door in Cadboro Bay. That just wouldn't do. Locals called the creature a sea hag because of the fear it inspired.

Quick-thinking newspaper editor Archie Willis embraced the beast as a local mascot. Perhaps he remembered the fame of Lake Okanagan's mysterious resident, the Ogopogo, and felt his quiet community could use a shake up. He sponsored a "name the monster" contest and declared "Cadborosaurus" the winner. The name was soon shortened to "Caddy." Sounds sort of like "cuddly," doesn't it? Soon after the name change, the creature was no longer feared by residents. The worse act it's been accused of since that day is swallowing a wounded duck in 1933.

Caddy's existence has been part of the folklore of the Chinook people for hundreds of years, but white settlers didn't spot it until the 1920s. Early sightings concluded that the creature was long (up to 30 metres) and thin, with two large flippers jutting out along its sides. Witnesses described its head as horselike, with a mane or jagged crest accentuating the long neck. Caddy's body arches in snakelike humps or coils that can be spotted as it speeds along Vancouver Island's east coast. On a bad day, Caddy's described as having a horrific face with well-defined nostrils and black eyes that cast a green glow. On a better day, it's described as a playful creature with a lovable face.

As with the Ogopogo, no biological evidence proves Caddy's existence, though that doesn't stop biologists, fans and pseudo-scientists from trying to dredge some up. In October 1937, the body of an apparent cadborosaurus was extracted from the belly of a sperm whale, farther up the coast. When unloaded at Naden Harbour whaling station in the Queen Charlotte Islands, the rotting body measured slightly over 3 metres long, with the famous horselike head. Three photos of the beast survive, yet somehow, the body—which could have proved beyond doubt the existence of such a creature—disappeared before any studies could commence. Coincidence, or the skillful work of a photographer and some large pieces of kelp?

Thanks to the work of marine scientists Paul LeBlond from the University of British Columbia and E.L. Bousfield from the Royal British Columbia Museum, Caddy can claim a scientific existence with the American Society of Zoologists since 1992. The society knows him as the *Cadborosaurus willsi*.

Bousfield and LeBlond have also reported that lucky Caddy has found himself a mate. Dubbed "Amy," an equally innocuous moniker, the pair now rules the waters of Cadboro Bay together. Amy is notoriously shy, with darker skin and no crest. Recent studies and reports by fisherman of smaller cadborosauri suggest that Caddy and Amy have produced offspring. Captian Bill Hagelund reported capturing one of the mini-Caddies (about 25 centimetres long) while fishing in Pirate's Cove. Hagelund inspected the creature enough to observe its fang-filled, spade-shaped jaw and fuzzy stomach but apparently was afraid of killing the creature, so he released it.

It appears that Caddy has taken to travel in his retirement, though he always returns to his home in the sheltered waters of Cadboro Bay. In 1996, there were over a dozen sightings of Caddy and, in June 1997, a crowd at Desolation Sound, in the middle of Vancouver Island's east coast was treated to a viewing. Maybe he'll pop up to the Okanagan soon to visit his famous cousin.

BIG

GARGANTUAN & RIDICULOUSLY OVERSIZED

With a Rod that Big, You Should See the Fish!

Small towns, especially ones that have to share a name with a much larger, more famous city, tend to be a little strange. To inflate their importance, some of these towns designate themselves the capital of something, no matter how trivial, misplaced or outdated the honour. Osoyoos became the "Spanish Capital of Canada," while Duncan proclaims to be the "Totem Capital." Houston, BC, once the tie-cutting centre of the Grand Truck Pacific Railway and forever in the shadow its famous southern cousin in Texas, describes itself as the "Steelhead Capital of Canada." Located between Prince Rupert and Prince George in the Bulkley Valley, Houston produces a pamphlet outlining more than two dozen steelhead fishing spots in the area, including Morice Lake and Collins Lake. Visitors realize just how small the town is (slightly over 4000 residents) when guidebooks recommend ambushing locals out for a morning coffee at the A &W as the "best source of day-to-day information on where the fish are biting." How better to celebrate being the capital of steelheads than to catch them? And how better to catch them than to use a giant fly rod—the world's largest fly rod. Warner Jarvis, a Houston local and avid fisherman, is behind the giant fly rod. Six Houston machine shops crafted the 20-metre-long, 363-kilogram rod out of aluminum and anodized bronze, to simulate graphite. Fundraising for the rod consisted of selling shares of the rod—you could purchase one centimetre of rod for a $5 share in the project. Strangely enough, fundraising began in the late 1980s, and shares remain available from the Houston Visitor Information Centre. Get yours quick before they're gone.

A Festival to
Call Our Own

*If you're in the mood to party, be it July, October or the
middle of a wet February, somewhere in British Columbia
a parade's just coming around the corner. Events that
celebrate local legends, folk music, chocolate, ska and wine
are just a starting point on the calendar of BC events.*

*For the dedicated celebrateur, British Columbia offers
eccentric festivals and parades for dead celebrities in
Victoria, sand sculptors in Harrison Hot Springs, ice carv-
ings and chili in Qualicum Beach, musical impersonators
in Whiskey Creek and "nothing at all" in Coombs.*

*Break out the fireworks and streamers,
it's time to party it up, BC-style.*

GRIZ DAYS
FERNIE

What to do with 875 centimetres of snowfall and a bunch of dummies?

Visitors headed to Fernie in early March could tell you that 6 metres of snow and a bunch of dummies are vital components of Griz Days, the week-long festival held in honour of the "Griz," a legendary mountain man who brings Fernie's massive amount of perfect powder from the skies each winter.

Any local will tell you that in 1879, the Griz was born inside the den of a grizzly. The town sent out a search party to investigate the strange noises heard that night—one man reported seeing a boy wearing a bearskin and hat. In later years, the Griz, no longer a child, was spotted in the hills above the Fernie Alpine Resort. He held a nearly 3-metre-long musket pointed to the sky to coax the snow to fall. The people of Fernie hold a festival in his honour to celebrate the snow. During the week-long winter party, the person who most resembles the famous mountain man is named honorary Griz for the rest of the year.

The town can generally expect 360 centimetres of snow each winter, and up on the ski hill, 875 centimetres.

The locals take their snowfall pretty seriously—and who can blame them. Winter tourists from BC, Alberta and the United States play an impressive role in town sustainability: service, lodging and tourism make up 34 percent of the local economy. No wonder the Griz gets such a welcoming party, with sporting events, competitions, parades and gatherings all week long.

The range of events suits all tastes, though I'm not positive the Griz would have been caught dead at a wine tasting or New Orleans—style cabaret. The extreme events seem much more his speed. A NASTAR (National Standards) race and obstacle course are held at the Fernie Alpine Resort.

As for the dummies, they're part of the annual Dummy Downhill, also hosted by the ski hill. Early on the big day, the Dummy Parade and weigh-in give the spectators a chance to view the competitors, all of whom must be between 90 and 180 centimetres long and no more than 90 centimetres wide. Unfortunately for the younger (or dummer) set, regulations stipulate that "no living cells" are allowed in the race. I guess I'll have to leave my 102-centimetre-long amoeba at home.

WHISKEY CREEK MUSIC FESTIVAL
WHISKEY CREEK

During the summer months especially, BC hosts so many music festivals that any new ones need to find a way to stand out. Some, such as Victoria's Ska Fest, celebrate newer forms of music, while others try to entice visitors with big-name lineups in remote locations. The Whiskey Creek Music Fest does neither; most of the performers aren't well known at all—as themselves, at least. That's because Whiskey Creek is a festival of musical impersonators.

In 2003, Bruce Macleod wanted to hold a concert to raise funds for local water system improvements. His son, Stuart, performed a show called *In Memory of the King*, a tribute to Elvis Presley. Originally, Stuart was the sole performer. He was soon joined by three other tribute artists, who performed the songs of Roy Orbison, Patsy Cline, Marty Robbins, Tammy Wynette and Neil Diamond. The Whiskey Creek Music Festival was born.

The second Festival, in 2004, added tributes to Shania Twain and Rod Stewart. Well-known tribute artists from all over North America agreed to travel to the small community near Qualicum Beach and Parksville on Vancouver Island to take part. To date, the festival has raised money for the water system, the Canadian Cancer Society and individual community members. Future recipients include the Coombs-Hillier Volunteer Fire department,

Arrowsmith Search and Rescue and environmental groups in the Whiskey Creek area.

The 11-hour-long musical extravaganza in 2006 featured tributes to Rod Stewart, Elvis Presley, Tina Turner, Bon Jovi and many more.

WRESTLING DAY
WILLIAMS LAKE

Some people will do just about anything to get their names on people's tongues, and I guess cities are the same. Williams Lake is just such a place. In most ways, the city is unremarkable, with just over 25,000 residents, a balance of local businesses and commercial chains, lots of recreation activities throughout the year and a Junior Hockey team, the Williams Lake Timberwolves.

So, like the gawky teenager it almost was back in the late 1930s (the city was founded in 1929), Williams Lake attempted to set itself apart. The story goes that two town merchants, Alistair Mackenzie and Syd Western, met for coffee on the cold afternoon of January 2. They both complained about the lack of people in their stores that day, chalking the slow business up to the late revelries of New Years Eve. The two men decided to close their shops and go home for the day. No doubt they were still feeling the holiday effects themselves. Mackenzie and Western phoned around to other businesses in town—there weren't that many at the time—and all agreed that the day would make a good holiday.

The name Wrestling Day was soon attached to the holiday, the reasoning being that if the day after Christmas was called Boxing Day, why not have a similar name for the day after New Years. Most of the town would be "wrestling" with a hangover that day, anyway.

Before 1943, Wrestling Day didn't amount to much more than a locally observed tradition. But that year, the Village Commission proclaimed Wrestling Day an official civic holiday.

Wrestling Day garnered no festivities, parades or celebrations of any kind. People simply stayed home and businesses stayed closed for one more day. A few people took part in a long walk down to Scout Island and back in an effort to do *something* to celebrate the day. Records don't indicate that anyone suggested a wrestling tournament. What a shame.

Mayor Tom Mason urged town council to abolish Wrestling Day in 1977, claiming that the town had "outgrown such nonsense." The chain stores were more to blame for Wrestling Day's cancellation than the stingy mayor. They, along with unionized lumber mills, didn't want to recognize the extra holiday. Citizens protested, and the holiday was reinstated the following year.

Today, as in its early years, nothing much happens on January 2 in Williams Lake. Some businesses open, others close. Some people stay home, others work. No one wrestles.

BIG GARGANTUAN & RIDICULOUSLY OVERSIZED

World's Largest Golf Ball

Between Dawson Creek and Fort St. John, in northern British Columbia, Taylor nestles in a scenic valley vastly different from the cold, hard scenery expected of the North. Besides the majestic Peace River, Taylor is home to a $40 million natural gas scrubbing plant and oil refinery, and the best corn in the valley. Thankfully, it hasn't yet erected a signing proclaiming itself the "Capital of Corn."

For anyone who loves the outdoors, Taylor offers great hiking and a challenging 18-hole golf course, described as the "Pride of the Peace." Besides a "peaceful" round of golf, visitors have the chance to see the world's largest golf ball. Converted from an old fuel tank, the ball is almost 13 metres in diameter and weighs in at 37 tonnes. That's definitely not PGA regulation size—and good luck getting a hole in one.

HARRISAND
HARRISON HOT SPRINGS

Harrison Hot Springs is a small village on Harrison Lake in the Fraser Valley. Internationally known for its mineral-rich local waters that reach temperatures of 40°C, the main attractions in Harrison Hot Springs are the commercial resorts with these naturally heated pools. In summer, though, many people would rather spend a day at the beach than in a hot spring. Harrison Lake is just the thing.

What I remember most about family trips to the beach is the inevitable building in the sand. We didn't always build castles; sometimes there were entire towns and skyscrapers embellished with shells and seaweed, or rude messages written out for siblings to see—only to be swept away by a wave before Mom and Dad got too close. I always thought of building sandcastles as one of those lazy family activities to be enjoyed for an afternoon then forgotten about when the tide came in. At Harrisand, the World Championship of Sand Sculpture Competition, I would have been laughed off the beach.

Actually, I wouldn't even have been able to get on the beach—the competition is open to Master Sand Sculptors *only*. For anyone who has absolutely no clue how one becomes an accredited Master Sand Sculptor, the term means:

☛ you've competed in the Master's category in Solo Competition at Québec City, Québec; South Padre Island, Texas; Virginia Beach, Virginia; Fort Myers, Florida or Imperial Beach, California

☛ or...you've competed as the Lead Sculptor of a Master's Team entered at Imperial Beach, California; Moscow, Russia; Scheveningen, Holland or Kaseda City, Japan

☛ or...you are an accomplished sculptor in another medium, such as bronze, ice, snow, terra cotta or wood *and* your work has won an award in juried shows or competitions *and* you can demonstrate considerable experience in sand sculpting

☛ or...you have worked with a professional sand sculpture company for at least three years and the lead sculptor of that company is prepared to acknowledge your competence and professionalism

I guess turning up with a pail and shovel is out of the question.

The Harrisand competition takes place in early September. Solo competitors and teams work for a week, then their creations remain on display into October. At the 2006 competition, sculptures ranged from a life-sized laughing Buddha and a slumbering giant to a knight on horseback in full armour.

FIRE AND ICE FESTIVAL
QUALICUM BEACH

The first weird feature of the Qualicum Beach Fire and Ice Festival is the date: the festival usually takes place on the first weekend in May each year. The irony of holding an ice sculpture festival near the beginning of summer must have been lost on the original event organizers. Qualicum Beach, 40 kilometres north of Raimondo on Vancouver Island's eastern coast, in a region where the average spring and summer temperatures reach 23°C.

The fire component of the Fire and Ice Festival is not fire carving but fire eating. Well, fire in the form of litre upon litre of chili, anyway. Teams of amateur and professional chefs present their take on this traditional Mexican dish to win awards and prizes, and to vie for the prestigious "Audience Favourite" award. More than 6000 visitors vote for this award each year.

In addition to the fire and ice, street performers dressed up as clowns, walking the street on stilts or performing daring fire tricks entertain the locals and visitors. For kids, the Jell-o carving event makes a tasty and entertaining challenge.

Why in the world anyone would want to celebrate summer with ice sculptures and chili is lost on me. Even in winter months (or fall or spring for that matter), this festival would be out of place. Maybe the idea was to use ice shavings to cool down the tasters' mouths after the chili contest, and someone started carving instead. More likely, a Qualicum Beach local suggested the festival as a joke, only to be surprised when the idea caught on.

I've got an idea for a Qualicum winter festival that's just as elemental: the Air and Water Festival: an eggplant parmigiana cook-off followed by a hot-air balloon race. See you there.

FESTIVAL OF MURALS
CHEMAINUS

Many Canadian towns that once thrived because of a gold rush or mining boom exist today in name only. Some are ghost towns or tourist centres, while others are merely blink-and-you'll-miss-'em stops along the highway.

At one time, Chemainus, in the Cowichan Valley of Vancouver Island, was a mill town, home to the largest covered-in sawmill in North America. Residents believed that the town's forestry sector would always thrive. That was not to be. In the early 1980s, the mill ran into financial difficulties and almost 20 percent (700 of 4000 people) became unemployed.

The North Cowichan council didn't want to let Chemainus fade away like so many other boom-to-bust towns. They decided to preserve the town in a new way, by turning it into the world's largest outdoor art gallery. The murals, to be displayed on businesses throughout the town, would be produced by local artists and would focus on a logging theme that celebrated the town's history.

Originating with just five murals in a worn-out downtown, the Chemainus Festival of Murals Society has expanded the "gallery" to 36 paintings, with a new one produced almost every year. Nearly a half-million visitors pass through Chemainus each year, making tourism the new number one industry. The majority of new businesses over the last 20 years have been bed and breakfasts, ice cream shops, gift shops and tour operators— some by horse and carriage.

In 1994 Chemainus won the British Airways Tourism for Tomorrow Award. This just goes to show what a little determination and stubbornness can do.

SNOW DAZE
PRINCE GEORGE

Known as BC's northern capital, Prince George is a busy city at the meeting of the Fraser and Nechako Rivers, with over 77,000 residents. A long-standing controversy over the Grand Trunk Pacific Railway's choice of the name Prince George for the community has yet to be resolved. In 1914, Grand Truck vice-president Morley Donaldson said the city had been named after the ruling King George V. But, before he was crowned, King George was actually Prince Edward, so the explanation seems unlikely.

In an internal company note written in December, 1911, Grand Trunk Pacific's president, Charles Hays, stated that the name Prince George had been chosen to ensure that the company's new town site was "permanently distinguished from the numerous towns now called Fort George, South Fort George, etc., which are in the vicinity" and also to make it clear that none of the other towns carried the company's endorsement.

In recent years a third explanation has arisen: the city was named after Prince George, the youngest brother of King George VI and the uncle of Queen Elizabeth II. Prince George named after a Prince George? Seems unlikely.

The controversy surrounding its name aside, Prince George holds an odd festival each winter. The festival is odd because instead of celebrating anything, the events, games and competitions are held near the end of January to relieve the locals' boredom and bring some excitement to the long winter.

In the 1970s, this festival was called the Prince George Winter Carnival. Also in the early 1970s, at the end of January, Prince George hosted the fledgling World Championship of Snow Golf tournament, a crazy tournament held in the snow featuring competitors in bizarre costumes. In its first few years of existence, the World Championship of Snow Golf exploded in popularity and gained national and international notoriety. Unfortunately, everyone realized how cold it could be to play a trudging sport like golf in sub-zero weather—or maybe someone just lost one too many golf balls in a snowdrift and gave up. In the mid 1970s, before the golf tournament dried up (or melted), Snow Golf and the Winter Carnival combined to form the "Mardi Gras of Winter."

Other popular events (some still part of the festival today) included Schmocky, Over-The-Line snowball, snow mobile and snow shoe races, snowman building and a Chow Mien eating contests. Wait a minute...one of these just doesn't fit in.

In the early 1980s, the term "snow daze" became part of the promotion of the winter Mardi Gras, and in 1995 it became the official name for the festival.

BIG GARGANTUAN & RIDICULOUSLY OVERSIZED

Mr. P.G.

As a recent addition to the Snow Daze festivities, Prince George holds a yearly Mr. Prince George Pageant. Perhaps this prestigious title comes from the town's enormous mascot, "Mr. Prince George," an 11.5-metre-high wooden man who stands at the junction of Highway 97 and Highway 16. In the early 1960s, "Mr. PG" could bow and speak, thanks to the loud speaker embedded in his nose. He visited the Kelowna Regatta, the Vancouver PNE Parade, Smithers and the Grey Cup Parade of 1963, where he won best float. Too bad the contestants today don't get to go on such a tour. Years have passed, but the days are never dull for Mr. PG. For CNIB (Canadian National Institute for the Blind) Week, he carries a cane and sports dark glasses, and at the end of the university year, in late spring, he wears a "Hire a Student" t-shirt, size XXXXXXL.

BRING OUT YOUR DEAD, UNO FESTIVAL OF SOLO PERFORMANCES
VICTORIA

Each summer, Victoria hosts solo performers from around the world at the annual Uno Festival of Solo Performances. Crowd favourites return from distances as far as Australia and England each year, but the festival also supports local talent and home-grown theatre companies. Enter Intrepid Theatre, self-subtitled as "Purveyors of Quality Alternative Theatre since 1986." When I think of "alternative" theatre—one-man-or-woman-show "alternative"—theatre, I immediately picture an angry, failed actor sitting alone on a wooden stool lit with a single spotlight, ranting about all the reasons he or she never made it.

Fortunately, my idea of alternative theatre is hopelessly incorrect. At *Bring Out Your Dead*, none of the performers rant about their failed careers because they're all celebrated actors, musicians, philosophers or literary personalities. It's really an A-List event. At the 2006 show, held in May, the six-feet-under lineup included film star Ava Gardner, opera-icon Maria Callas, comedienne Lucille Ball, Canadian writer Stephen Leacock, Nazi propaganda starlet Renata Miller, comedienne Gracie Allen and comedian Andy Kaufman.

Bring Out Your Dead emerged from a theatre exercise, where actors immersed themselves in the character of a celebrity by performing monologues as that person. The results were so entertaining that Intrepid Theatre decided to bring the monologues to the stage. Not wanting the audience to miss out on the fun, the company encourages everyone to attend dressed as their favourite dead celebrity. Free admission to the show and other prizes up the temptation to come fully costumed. Watch out, though, because anyone dressed up becomes fair game for impromptu sketches, competitions and games. In *Hot Seat*, another theatre-school inspiration, actors and audience members must answer a series of "general knowledge" questions while in character. While Judy Garland (dressed as Dorothy of Oz, of course) may be easy to distinguish, just what gets construed as "general knowledge" seems a bit suspect. I'm not sure I'd recognize Greek philosopher Epicurus no matter how accurate the costume.

FESTIVAL OF THE TOMATO
OLIVER

Self described as the "Wine Capital of Canada," Oliver is home to 10 percent of our country's wineries and 61 percent of BC's grape-growing acreage. The majority of these vineyards and wineries can be spotted from a drive down the "Golden Mile," just south of the town centre. No one would be surprised to learn that Oliver hosts the Festival of the Grape each summer—nothing weird about that. Oliver's lesser-known foodie festival is perhaps a bit more odd: Festival of the Tomato, a day-long party filled with competitions and silly events, celebrates all that's red, ripe and tasty...but not a grape. The festival grounds at Covert Farms used to be a vineyard which, according to the website, "made consistently unremarkable Château Okanagan River Channel wines."

Every September, families travel to Covert Farms dressed in their Sunday worst to experience a myriad of alternative tomato activities. Imagine tomato mini-golf through fields of knee-high alfalfa. Or tomato bocce ball—how they tell the competitors apart is a mystery to me. I'm imagining team games of *ripe* versus *unripe*, though I suspect the green tomato teams would have a distinct accuracy advantage. I'm no expert, though; I've never had the pleasure of playing. The eating aspect of tomatoes satisfies me.

For the brave—or just those who don't mind getting dirty— there is the tomato catapult and slingshot contest or a very saucy game of tug-of-war. The losers end up in pile of ripe tomatoes. The day concludes with the annual tomato fight.

For anyone who likes their tomatoes on their plate, not their body, the Iron Tomato Chef Competition features local chefs from many of the restaurants in Oliver and its neighbouring town at the south end of the Golden Mile, Osoyoos. Local microbreweries and wineries sell beer and wine (and offer tastings) throughout the day. My guess is that half the participants in the tomato fight had been "sampling" these local beverages for most of the afternoon.

The Covert family donates produce each year to the Gleaners— an organization that dries local fruits and vegetables, then makes soup and other products to be shipped to needy communities around the world. Any culls (produce that doesn't meet specific guidelines) goes back to the farm to be used as fertilizer...or weapons in the tomato fight. The two farm pigs, Gala and Ambrosia, get to clean up after the festival.

Fan Tan Alley

Half a block from the elaborate golden lions of the Gates of Harmony, surrounded by produce markets, coffee shops and specialty boutique stores, hides Fan Tan Alley, Canada's narrowest street and the heart of its oldest Chinatown. At its narrowest point, the alley measures less than one metre wide, but even at its widest, only young children could lie across it comfortably. The worn, red bricks on the walls are nearly unchanged since Chinatown's earliest days; coded signs to local gambling and opium dens are still visible to those who know where to look. The alley's narrow space, made even more eerie by the dramatic, three-storey height of the brick buildings, must have suited the shadowy types who conducted their business here.

Fan Tan Alley must have been a hopping place in its heyday, at the end of the 19th century. It wouldn't have taken many people to make the 61-metre-long alley feel packed, and hordes of Chinese immigrants frequented the 12 gambling houses and restaurants tucked between Fisguard Street and Pandora Avenue. Workers often lost their entire day's pay in a few hours of betting, and possessions changed hands when money ran out. Opium addiction arose largely because of the racism of the Canadian government at the time. While addiction quickly surfaced in the Chinese communities, the government did not regard it as a social issue because it destroyed the lives of the immigrants. Also, the government profited from the sales of licence fees to sell the drug. Though the opium problem was largely ignored, the government heavily monitored gambling houses. An old peephole that was used to screen visitors wanting to play the illegal games of mah jong, dominoes and fan tan still exists on the right-hand wall heading toward Fisguard Street. Fan tan refers to a gambling game from China. *Fan* means "to turn

☞

BIG GARGANTUAN & RIDICULOUSLY OVERSIZED over" (in the game, a cup) and *tan* means "to spread out" (in the game, a pile of buttons). It's a simple game to play—and purely a matter of chance. The croupier (or "dealer,") grabs a handful of buttons and places them on a board. He quickly covers the pile with the cup, and the betting begins. The players must bet on a number: one, two, three or four, by placing their stakes on a designated area of a board. When the cup is uncovered, the buttons are removed from the pile in groups of four until no more groups can be taken. If one button remains, the dealer pays to those who bet "one," and so on. The game seems simplistic, but many men lost their paycheques, their goods or even their lives over it. Perhaps, delirious on opium or just drunk, fan tan was the most challenging game some of these men were capable of playing.

For men who could resist the temptation of gambling, booze and opium, the Chinese opera players performed here, along with acrobats brought up from San Francisco. Finding a way to put on any type of performance in the tiny space would have been remarkable—but acrobatics? More like contortionists! Soon, the acrobats weren't the only San Franciso export in Fan Tan Alley. American entrepreneurs sent prostitutes to work in Chinatown's many brothels. Many of the original "bad houses" still stand; one's a popular bakery and breakfast spot for present-day Victoria residents.

Authentic signs of Chinatown's history survive in Fan Tan Alley. The Chinatown Trading Company, a mazelike store winding though many small, dark rooms, displays historical opium pipes and dice, and sells wooden fans, figurines, bamboo furniture and small toys.

PACIFIC NORTHWEST ELVIS FESTIVAL
PENTICTON

The town motto of Penticton reads "A Place to Live Forever," a translation of its native Salish name. Many visitors to this quiet city during the long summer months have probably uttered similar sentiments. The Okanagan, with its lush valley orchards, plethora of lakes and activities for outdoor enthusiasts, is consistently ranked as one of the best places in Canada to live. Each June, Penticton becomes a place for the King to live forever, as the city becomes home to hordes (nearly 18,000 in 2005) of Elvis tribute artists, fans and look-alikes covering all the Elvis personas—young rockabilly Elvis, hip-shaking Elvis and chunky Disco Elvis. Yup, for three days, Penticton becomes the pomade and sideburn capital of the world.

Many people report Elvis sightings each year—how many of these take place in Penticton has not been documented. There are more than 25,000 Elvises worldwide. Extreme Elvis behaves as the King might if he were alive today—he lets fans rub his belly and has upset Elvis fans by stripping on stage, using the catchphrase, "Every generation gets the Elvis it deserves." Elvis Herselvis is a drag King from San Francisco. El Vez, or "gay Mexican Elvis" performers punk versions of Elvis hits. And who can leave out the Flying Elvi, a 10-member group of skydiving Elvises who can be hired to drop in on parties and special events.

Fans at the Penticton Festival prefer their Elvises a bit more traditional. Elvis Tribute Artists take part in judged competitions as they compete to be named professional and amateur champions. Along with the judged performances, fans can attend the gospel showcase on the Sunday of the Festival or meet celebrity guests from Elvis's life.

Saturday night is the highlight for most visitors, with a rockin' party filled by more pelvis-shaking dancers than you'll find anywhere else. If nothing else, Penticton certainly is a place where Elvis can stay forever, if he ever gets tired of Graceland.

VANCOUVER ISLAND PUMPKIN FEST
LADYSMITH

Ladysmith, a small community on Vancouver Island's east coast, was named, indirectly, after the wife of Lieutenant General Harry Smith, who established the town of Ladysmith in South Africa before the Boer War.

Ladysmith, BC, was established during the peak mining days on Vancouver Island. With over 15 hotels, many businesses and even a house of ill repute, Ladysmith seemed destined to ride the coal wave forever. A series of blasts that killed over 30 people followed by a mining strike withered the coal industry, but soon, forestry brought the town back to life.

With a rich mining and forestry history, Ladysmith seems the perfect place for a logger sports or "mining days" festival. These events do occur, but the festival that really shakes the town up is Pumpkinfest, held every October.

Over the Thanksgiving long weekend, a variety of pumpkin-related events roll into town, including the construction of the world's largest pumpkin pie. The biggest one yet, "baked" in 2003, measured in at a tasty 12 metres long by 1.2 metres wide.

Apparently, the whole town gets into the spirit of the weekend by decorating front lawns, windowsills and the backs of trucks with the bright orange deities. The festival concludes with the paddling of a giant pumpkin in the harbour.

PARADE OF THE LOST SOULS
VANCOUVER

Anyone who feels that Vancouver has become too commercial, with a Starbucks on every corner, new apartments or condos in never-ending construction and Hollywood celebrities calling it their "Up North" home, probably hasn't passed Commercial Drive at Halloween.

Fortunately, the Parade of the Lost Souls hearkens back to ancient celebrations of Halloween and the Day of the Dead, when the souls of those who had died during the year were allowed access into the "land of the dead." The Parade of the Lost Souls is an attempt to regain some of the significance of these seasonal celebrations and hopes to awaken that spirit in the minds of Vancouverites each October. The neighbourhood celebration tries to "honour the dead, wake the living and overcome our fears."

The event has become hugely popular since 1993, its inaugural year. Initially a neighbourhood celebration that provided a fun alternative to trick-or-treating from door to door, the night now draws crowds nearing 20,000. In 2005, organizers took a one-year hiatus to rethink public safety, the choice of venue and the addition of new elements.

On celebration night, always in the final days of October but not necessarily Halloween, creepy stilt-walkers, bloody-faced creatures, moaning ghosts and skeletons troop through the residential neighbourhood of Commercial Drive. Yards are littered with pumpkins and burning torches, casting an eerie glow over the paraders. Drums beat in ominous rhythms, and the occasional accordion player makes the scene sound more like an old horror film than a Vancouver celebration.

On corners, under streetlights that have been altered with red filters, musicians huddle with guitars, adding a touch of punk to the festivities. I picture the streets looking something like the sets of that horrible 1980's movie *Little Monsters*, in which Howie Mandel pulled a prepubescent Fred Savage under his bed into a world of undead, mohawked teens with horns and drinking problems.

Following the parade, the mass of ghouls tramps to an open field where the organized entertainment begins. Bikes with flaming spokes circle each other on stages 2 metres up, and fire dancers perform for cheering crowds. At least this aspect of Vancouver spirit can be resurrected once each year.

SEAFEST
ALERT BAY

The village of Alert Bay is located at the top of Johnstone Strait on Cormorant Island, a 5-kilometre-long island shaped like a croissant. Known as "Home of the Killer Whale," Alert Bay is a long-established community that once served as a trading post for the First Nations people and mariners from abroad. The island was named after a coastal cruiser, the HMS *Cormorant* in 1846. Alert Bay derived its name from the HMS *Alert*, which was stationed on the island's northwest coast in 1858. The 'Namgis First Nations Burial Ground marks the centre of the village, near world's tallest totem pole. You'd think with a community so steeped in First Nations culture—something most British Columbians known disgracefully little about—the most talked about festival in town would be related to the village's history. It's not.

Alert Bay's SeaFest consists of gameshow-esque events such as Family Feud, the SeaFest Cabaret, a Strong Man/Strong Woman competition, a baby contest and the crowning of Mr. and Mrs. SeaFest. All this festival needs is a booming-voiced announcer to adjudicate the lip-syncing competition. "Next up, ladies and gentlemen, these singers will be competing for a shopping spree at the Shop Rite!" Really—that's an event.

Even the Shop Rite Shopping Spree fails to capture the title of strangest SeaFest event. To add to the television quality of the festival, those with the know-how can enter the "Golden Girls Crochet Contest." Whether or not Betty White plans on attending this year remains to be seen.

SeaFest takes place near the end of August. The community can be reached by taking the ferry from Port McNeil on Vancouver Island.

World's Largest Cherry Pie

Oliver takes its name from "Honest" John Oliver, who served as one of British Columbia's premiers after World War I. Honest John owned a farm in Delta, BC, and believed the south end of the Okanagan could prosper as a fruit growing region. But what to do about the extreme heat and lack of water? Honest John's liberal government sponsored the South Okanagan Lands Project, through which an irrigation canal was built to keep the land lush and green throughout the dry summers. Osoyoos and Oliver in particular benefited from the advanced irrigation system, transforming from arid desert into a fertile, fruit-growing land.

In 1990, some very hungry citizens in Oliver baked the world's largest cherry pie. The pie weighed 17,106 kilograms and had to be baked in a pit 11 metres in diameter for 6.5 hours. What a fitting testament to the amount of fruit the valley produces.

NATURAL FIBRE FESTIVAL
SALT SPRING ISLAND

Salt Spring Island is the largest of the Gulf Islands, tucked between Vancouver and Victoria. Once used as part of a route for escaped slaves from the United States, Salt Spring now draws attention for its prospering sheep farms, artisans, local wines and cheeses. For years, the island has been home to many craftspeople, artists and wanna-be artists; visitors who ferry over for the weekly Saturday market can attest to the abundance of local produce (both art and food) that flourish on Salt Spring.

As long as the island has been a haven for artists, it's been fodder for jokes about tree-hugging hippies and an over-fondness for granola and anything "natural." It's the type of place easterners think of when they joke about the West Coast.

Island residents set on dispelling this reputation probably don't attend the Natural Fibre Festival, an annual celebration of fibres and locally made products. Those who do attend, however, can take part in hands-on fibre arts demonstrations and visit the barns to meet the different varieties of fleece animals and watch fabrics being spun, woven and knit. Farm tours are available, too, if that much fibre isn't enough!

For those accustomed to more tradition festivals, the equivalent here to, say, any sporting competition, is the Sheep-to-Shawl. Teams of four spinners and one weaver race to card and spin yarn, then complete a lengthy shawl—all in six hours. Whew! Talk about exhilarating entertainment! For a more viewer-friendly excursion, the fashion show features clothing made from the fleece of local animals and designed by locals, too.

Other festival highlights include demonstrations with processing tools, shearing demos and a twig chair workshop.

MIDSUMMER NIGHT'S PARADE
COOMBS

A popular tourist destination on Vancouver Island, Coombs is filled with heritage buildings and gift shops waiting for guests. In the early years of the 20th century, the Salvation Army sponsored an immigration program that brought nearly a quarter of a million poor English and Welsh people to Canada. Many came to Vancouver Island. Around 1910, a handful of these families established the village of Coombs, located 9 kilometres west of Parksville on Vancouver Island, and named it after the Army's Canadian Commissioner, Captain Thomas Coombs. One would expect a village founded by English and Welsh immigrants, and named after a soldier, to be either quaintly British or designed with military precision. Coombs is neither.

A plaque once found on a wall in Coombs read:

"There ain't no place like this place, near the place, so this must be the place".

The plaque is now gone, but the sentiment of the message still rings true today. While several heritage buildings still stand in the village centre, Coombs is best known for its local craft outlets, its mini golf, the World Parrot Refuge and the Coombs County Market. But the weirdest thing of all in Coombs is the annual Midsummer Night's Parade, a celebration of...well...nothing much at all.

For most of the summer, Old West activities take over the village. Why? Don't ask me. Vancouver Island locals are more likely to be found wearing fleece and Birkenstocks than leather cowboy boots, but nevertheless, Bull-O-Rama, a fiddle jamboree, a bluegrass festival and a two-day rodeo bring cowboy spirit to the small Vancouver Island community.

The Midsummer Night's Parade features music and entertainment throughout the day, a contest to find the "Chicken

Chuckin' Champion"—the person who successfully throws
a rubber chicken at a series of targets—and something called
"Hillbilly Horses."

The games and contests are so bizarre that they take the focus off
of the actual reason for the event. Not that it's hard to do: there
really isn't any reason for it at all. The *real, extended* name of the
parade is the "Just for the Heck of it, No Reason at All,
Midsummer Night's Parade." Now that's a mouthful.

Just a thought: Considering that most people think of late
August as the end, not middle of summer, the organizers should
change the parade title to the "Just for the Heck of it, No
Reason at All, Mid-but-sort-of-late-Summer Cowboy Festival for
Island Folk." That's got a nice ring to it.

We Are What We Eat

*Around the world, regions distinguish their local flavour
with cultural delicacies and traditional foods.*

*In British Columbia, we have salmon and the Nanaimo
bar, a three-layer bar that doesn't even need to be baked.
With a regional dish composed mainly of cold custard, it's no
wonder British Columbians have adopted more exotic tastes.*

*BC is home to Canada's only banana plantation and one
of the world's most expensive loaves of bread.
Readers, I hope you're hungry...*

THE PATH
QUEEN CHARLOTTE ISLANDS

When I first heard rumours about a restaurant in the Queen Charlotte Islands that prepared all its dishes without electricity, I wondered how the California craze for raw-food diets had managed to make it up north without catching on in the rest of BC. I was quickly assured that this wasn't the case, but The Path restaurant remains a bit of a mystery to me. The restaurant doesn't just shun hydro for cooking; it is entirely electricity-free. Guests dine on the house specialties—predominantly vegetarian and local seafood dishes—by the glow of kerosene lamps. How romantic— just like a fishing trip.

Most people know the Queen Charlotte Islands for their exquisite Native artwork and first-rate wilderness adventures on the islands' sunny fields, endless beaches and treacherous waters. Because of their remote location, the Queen Charlottes have remained relatively untouched by commercial development pressure. The islands' population includes a high number of "back-to-the-land" types. Surely one of them came up with the idea for The Path restaurant.

Self-described as "beyond the reach of hydro and within touch of Mother Nature," The Path is known locally for its terrific desserts. The decor matches the laid-back, West-Coast model you'd expect: driftwood benches under the tables, kerosene lamps creating a campfire atmosphere—I hope smores are on the menu. Saturday nights feature jam sessions after dinner, so the staff encourages visitors to bring their guitars, fiddles, drums and musical spirit to dinner. Just leave the amp at home.

FERNANDES FRUIT STAND
OSOYOOS

Osoyoos is hot. The southernmost town in the Okanagan
Valley, Osoyoos composes the tip of the Sonora Desert, the only
desert in Canada, home to creatures such as yellow-bellied
marmots, pygmy horned toads and the Calliope hummingbird.
And watch out for the rattlesnakes! Generally, deserts are defined
as areas that receive, on average, less than 25 centimetres of rain
per year. Osoyoos comes in well under the mark, at a measly 20
centimetres annually.

Osoyoos boasts the lowest rainfall, highest temperatures and warmest lake in Canada. During summer, temperatures average 38°C. Picturesque orchards and vineyards line the outskirts of town. Tourists pour into the Okanagan Valley during summer, more than quadrupling Osoyoos's winter population of under 5000 residents.

Translated from Inkaneep, the local Native dialect, *osoyoos* means "narrowing of the waters" or "sandbar across." People driving or cycling down into Osoyoos from either Anarchist Mountain on the east or Richter Pass on the west won't need much time to see why. Through the centre of Osoyoos Lake, a sandbar stretches nearly all the way across, making a "walk" across the lake a unique summer activity. Just watch out for the boats! Originally named "Soo-Yoos," an "o" was apparently added to lend the name a more dignified sound.

The ideal weather allows for the longest growing season in Canada. Osoyoos produces a myriad of fruits, including cherries, apricots, peaches, plums, strawberries, raspberries, nectarines, apples, watermelon, blueberries and, of course, grapes. The weather becomes so hot in summer that at one time, Osoyoos boasted Canada's only banana plantation. Bananas in Canada? In the land of snow and ice? Who would have guessed?

One account of the Osoyoos banana plantation claims that a banana tree was given as a gift to a local farmer named Fernando. He nurtured the plant, then planted more, creating Canada's first and only banana farm, which is now a fruit market. Inspired by Fernando's work, Bonnie and Gordon Turnbull of Saskatchewan moved to Osoyoos and set up a juice bar. They called it the "Big Banana Juice and Smoothie Bar" after the plantation's success.

A nice story, to be sure. But not much of it could be called the truth.

Fernandes Fruit Market actually began when Joe and Maria Fernandes emigrated from Madeira, Portugal, to Osoyoos in 1959. After planting a successful orchard, Joe longed to grow the sugar cane, bananas and other tropical fruit he remembered from Portugal. The climate seemed about right, so he decided to give it a try. In 1980, Joe built the only banana farm in Canada. Inside his hothouse, over 500 banana trees, sugar cane, lemon and orange trees and many other exotic plants flourished. On July 15 of each year, Joe opened the hothouse to the curious eyes of his neighbours and tourists. The fruit market gave away free bananas that day too. After Joe's death, the banana farm closed. The Fruit Stand continues to grow, now in the hands of Joe and Maria's seven children: Helen, Laura, Lucy, Joe, Cidalia, Tom and Greg. The Big Banana Juice Bar does exist, but it opened after the banana plantation closed.

URBAN FARE
YALETOWN, VANCOUVER

Vancouver's Yaletown district was once filled with warehouses.
The name stems from the railway workers from Yale, BC, who
lived in the area during the early 1900s. Yaletown's taste has
changed over the years; it's now the spot to be seen in Vancouver.
The "light industrial district" hides legendary nightclubs and
hip boutique hotels such as Opus. At the other end of Yaletown,
a clean residential neighbourhood houses yuppies in high-rise
apartment buildings and condos.

For all the specialty and designer shops that pack the streets of
Yaletown, the strangest store has got to be Urban Fare, a grocery

store that strives to "cater to every epicurean delight." Now, I've got nothing against "foodies," but Urban Fare takes fancy eating to a whole new level of wow. And nowhere is the wow-factor more evident than the store's expansive bakery.

At my local BigName grocery store chain, the most expensive bread in the case is an olive-and-cheese-stuffed loaf for $5.99. It's delicious, so sometimes I splurge.

At Urban Fare, I'm sure you can find a loaf of bread for $5.99, but the *bread du jour* most definitely is the imported Poilâne, at $40 per loaf. If you want a decorated loaf (stamped with the bakery name), the price jumps to $85. Isn't bread just flour, water and salt?

The bread does have a fascinating story. Pierre l'Ermite, a preacher, rode though the towns of Normandy in the late 11th century, allowing locals to grab hairs from his horse as he passed to use as religious icons. The region became known as "Poilgris" (grey hairs), which later changed to "Poils de l'âne" (donkey's hairs) and finally just Poilâne. Centuries later, in 1925, Pierre Poilâne travelled to France and Italy to learn about baking. After his return, he opened a bakery using the ancestral methods he had been taught abroad.

Frank Sinatra was known to buy the famous bread, as is Robert De Niro. But it's a gentleman in New York who can claim to be the bread's biggest fan: in 1997, he paid Poilâne $100,000 to ensure that his children and grandchildren receive a loaf every week for life.

Just a thought: doesn't it seem ironic that a man who made his bread famous by using ancestral baking methods would agree to Fed-Ex his product around the world?

If you're on a low-carb diet, don't despair. Urban Fare offers plenty of pricey, exotic foods flown in from around the world. How about a square watermelon from Japan for $82? They may defy logic, but hey, so does buying them!

CABLE HOUSE CAFÉ
SAYWARD

Located on the east side of the one-lane bridge on Sayward Road, the Cable Cook House combines Sayward's two most important industries, logging and tourism. No, the owners don't let tourists loose in the forest with chainsaws, but the tourists can have a tasty meal in one of the island's most interesting restaurants.

Sayward is located about one hour north of Campbell River on the northeast shore of Vancouver Island. If you're getting close to Sayward and your stomach begins to rumble, there really is only one place to stop. The building itself is part of Sayward's logging history. Created from remnants of the logging industry, the site is also home to retired logging equipment. Builder Glen Duncan made the building from a steel frame, then covered the walls with old logging cable, used to haul logs through the bush and over the river. To complete the structure, he needed 2500 metres of cable, which would weigh in the vicinity of 26 tonnes.

On the building's exterior, Duncan left the cables rusty to preserve authenticity. Inside, though, he sandblasted to remove the rust from the cables, then coated them with Polylite and painted them with a mixture of bronze powder and varnish. Glen and his wife, Fran, opened the restaurant in 1970, and it's still today known for hearty meals and the best pie on northern Vancouver Island.

THE TOMAHAWK RESTAURANT
NORTH VANCOUVER

In this time of low-carb, low-fat, raw-food diets, it's nice to know that fast-food joints aren't the only places left to find old-fashioned burgers and fries. Of course, at the Tomahawk Restaurant, everything's done with a bit of BC flair.

Chick Chamberlain, the Tomahawk Restaurant's founder, opened his first small coffee shop in 1926 in what is now Heywood Park in North Vancouver. He soon rented a larger space on Marine Drive, which became the legendary Tomahawk Barbeque. Guest could sit at the counter on one of the 14 stools or wait in their cars for Chick to run out to take their order. He admitted later that the dusty gravel roads back then made the drive-in a less-than-convenient place to eat. He also admitted that, back in those days, he didn't really know how to cook. But he grew his own mushrooms, made his own pickles and milk-shake syrups and raised his own chickens.

Despite his lack of experience, the customers came in droves for Chick's Yukon Breakfast and huge burgers, which he named after chiefs in British Columbia: Skookum Chief, Chief Capilano, Chief Raven, Chief Dominic Charlie, Chief August Jack. The burgers were so huge that patrons claimed to get "meat drunk" after finishing one.

During the Depression, when money was tight, Chick often traded his food for crafts or goods. He had soon amassed a collection of handmade pots, drums, cooking utensils, totem poles and masks that most people would have considered to be of little value. Today his collection is of great historical importance; the artifacts decorate the restaurant's new location at 1550 Phillip Avenue.

Chick's son and grandson now run the Tomahawk. They proudly serve up the restaurant's specialties, the Yukon Breakfast and "meat drunk" burgers. As an added bonus, at the end of the meal, patrons now receive free headdresses that remind me of the paper crowns Burger King used to distribute with its kid meals. The Tomahawk's headdresses are infinitely cooler.

THE SCOTCH BAKERY
NANAIMO

The Scotch Bakery, on Commercial Street in downtown Nanaimo, claims to be the home of the Nanaimo bar. I'm sure a few bakeries would like to dispute that claim. In fact, little evidence exists to prove that Nanaimo is even the true home of the famous triple-layer dessert.

According to one legend, the Harewood Ladies' Auxiliary found the recipe in the *Vancouver Sun* in the 1950s, under the name "Chocolate Fridge Cake." The ladies renamed the treat and placed it in their fundraiser cookbook. No record of the *Vancouver Sun* article has been found. Other stories suggest that thoughtful mothers in Northern England shipped the sugary treat to their coal-miner sons in Nanaimo. Still other stories say that Dutch settlers brought the recipe to Vancouver Island in the early 1900s.

No matter how it arrived, the recipe seems to have travelled throughout BC with the wives of workers in the company towns of the 1950s.

The Scotch Bakery and the city of Nanaimo take the bars very seriously. I've heard that at one time, the city's official mascot was "Nanaimo Barney," a giant stuffed Nanaimo bar. But like most things Nanaimo bar—related, there's no proof. Even I have a hard time believing this one. A city adopting a chocolate-custard dessert as its official mascot? That's a stretch, even for BC.

In 1986, Mayor Graeme Roberts held a contest to find the ultimate Nanaimo bar recipe. Joyce Hardcastle won in a unanimous vote from the lucky judges. The city information centre hands out official copies of her winning recipe.

Blossoming Boot

In March 1778, when he stepped into Friendly Cove on Nootka Island, Captain James Cook became the first European visit British Columbia. The natives yelled *itchme nutka*—go around—to guide Cook's ship, but Cook believed they were calling out the name of the land. For these reasons, Nootka sound is known as the birthplace of British Columbia. Gold River lies in the heart of Nootka Sound, between Strathcona Provincial Park and the Great Lands of the Maquinna, about 70 kilometres north of Tofino. The name "Gold River" comes directly from the 1860s, when the village was established as a resource town. When a town centre was finally built in 1965, Gold River became Canada's first all-electric town and the first to incorporate underground wiring. The town's primary industry gradually shifted to forestry, which I hope explains the relevance of the town's giant, blossoming boot. Yes, the boot acts a planter for flowers each spring and summer. I'm thinking that the local blooms were the loggers' take on Odor-Eaters! Local chainsaw carver Lee Yateman carved the boot from a single piece of wood in 2001, and the town has celebrated it with a Blossoming Boot Festival even since. Town residents create planters from their old boots to be judged in a Blossoming Boot Contest.

Island Time

The islands that line British Columbia's coast constitute some of Canada's last uncommercialized land, even though they were some of the first "touched" by European expansion.

Marked by tragedy and failed Utopias, the islands that dot the waters of the Pacific somehow remain tranquil. These are the communities where a relaxed attitude is the norm. A typical weekend activity consists of kayaking and picnic lunches, not fast food and the mall.

When life gets too hectic, consider taking in a little "island time."

SOINTULA
MALCOLM ISLAND

Sointula is the main settlement on Malcolm Island, a large island between Vancouver Island and the British Columbia mainland. This "Inside Passage" of water runs from the Alaska border down to Victoria and is notorious for its unpredictable waters and wild storms. Malcolm Island is located 7 kilometres off the coast of Port McNeil. The area known as the North Island is sparsely populated, and Sointula could hardly be described as busy. When you get off the ferry, locals are happy to tell you that if you want a quick tour of the village, "Go left." If you want a longer walk, past the cemetery and down to the shore, "Go right."

Sointula's present population is partly made up of descendants of the Island's first inhabitants. When Europeans moved to Canada to escape political and economic turmoil at the turn of the 20th century, a group of Finnish idealists, known as the Kalevan Kansa, established a socialist community on Malcolm Island. A community based on the concept of communal property, equal rights for women, shared work and shared rewards. A community based on *sointula*, a Finnish term for "harmony."

The idealized Sointula ran into problems faced by the many Utopian communities founded on the West Coast: financial debt mounted from the purchase of the property from the BC government; inexperience farming the island's terrain; problems between community members and the unofficial leader; and one devastating disaster. For Sointula, this disaster came in the form of a fire that destroyed the communal centre. Eleven people died, and most of the supplies and records were burned, proving that as well as rewards, hardship would be shared by all, too.

Following the "failed Utopia" pattern, Kurikka, the community leader, left the island with his remaining disciples, leaving the financial burden on those that stayed behind. This could have meant the end of Sointula, but it was really just the beginning.

The dedicated families that stayed rebuilt, sold all but their own plots back to the government and turned to commercial fishing.

Sointula after the turn of the 21st century remains a peaceful, quiet community, rich in the little quirks that mark any small town. For example: the Co-op store is closed all day Sunday—and sometimes on Wednesday afternoons; you need to make an appointment to visit the museum; the 8:00 am ferry leaves at 7:20 am on Sundays; and if you're driving, watch out for dogs fast asleep on the road.

TLELL
QUEEN CHARLOTTE ISLANDS

A visit to Tlell, a smallish community (375 people) concentrated on the east of coast of Graham Island, feels like stepping back in time to the 1960s. The wooden sides of most of the ramshackle homes and stores have been adorned with painted sunbursts and rainbows. People who make the journey to Tlell awe over the dramatic northern scenery. The air smells of the sea or the forests, depending on the weather, and the easy meadows suddenly become sharp rock faces near the ocean. Tlell's claim to fame these days rests mainly on the success of the Edge of the World Music Festival, a summer event that embraces all kinds of music, from ska to bluegrass, rap to afrobeat, rock to reggae.

Like the festival, Tlell's growth as a village has a "counter culture" element to it. The first homesteader in the region was a man named William Thomas Hodges, a swarthy man who looked like a pirate. He carried pistols and wore his long, dark hair pulled into a tight ponytail. "Mexican Tom," as he came to be known, apparently liked to enthrall the people he came across in his journeys with stories of his home country. One problem—he wasn't Mexican.

Mexican Tom's fighting attitude led him to be exiled from some of the towns he briefly settled in, such as Hazelton and Masset. It's astounding he didn't lose his life—in Masset, locals spotted him rounding up the cattle of George Rudge, the hotel keeper in Port Simpson. Mexican Tom eventually settled in Tlell, which was little more than grass, rock and forest back in 1904. And what was the first thing he wanted after he settled? A wife. Pickings were pretty slim in those days, so the bachelor enlisted the help of some well-written friends. Through lonely-hearts advertisements, and the romantic penmanship of his friends, Tom convinced Flora Burns, a widow from Seattle, to head north. For another somewhat creepy BC—Cyrano de Bergerac connection, check out the Nelson Murals. It's unclear whether Mexican Tom suffered the misfortune of a large nose. Flora arrived at Skidegate, 43 kilometres south of the Tom's ranch, in 1907. The couple was married by the ship's captain on the night of Flora's arrival. To the disappointment of his friends, the marriage between Mexican Tom and American Flora didn't last. Not because the couple had problems, but because Tom died in Prince Rupert on November 23, 1912.

World's Largest Burl

In tree lingo, for anyone not in-the-know, a burl is an outgrowth on a tree. The rounded growth looks like a giant knot and is often used to create artwork and wood veneers. In some tree species, such as redwoods, burls can grow to be larger than a person, or even into new redwood trees. Port McNeil, the centre of logging activity on northern Vancouver Island, boasts not only the world's largest burl, but the second largest, too. The bigger of the two weighs 22 tonnes and measures nearly 14 metres around. That's one big burl.

ECHO BAY PRIVATE MUSEUM
ECHO BAY

What do you do if you can't bear to throw anything away, but your home can't accommodate any more stuff? Collect everything together in one room, call it a museum, and charge admission! At least, that worked for Billy Proctor of Echo Bay.

Tucked on the north side of Gilford Island, in the Broughton Archipelago, Echo Bay provides water and overnight camping to the many sea kayakers who paddle the gentle waters off northeastern Vancouver Island.

Like most of northern Vancouver Island, Echo Bay has a rich First Nations history. The Kwakiutl First Nations have lived in the area for thousands of years; many pictographs and burial sites survive today. Besides these natural wonders, tourist attractions are sparse. Except, of course, for the Echo Bay Private Museum.

At the Echo Bay Private Museum, Billy Proctor displays the "junk" he collected during his years as a fisherman and beachcomber. He was born in a shack in the woods surrounding Port Neville and has called many of the remote islands and bays in the area home. His "junk" consists mainly of animal traps, skinning boards, logging equipment and hundreds of old empty bottles. Some of the rarer items are bone and rock artifacts, some of which date back 8000 years. My storage room is getting pretty full—maybe I should follow Proctor's lead and open the first Victoria Private Museum of Used Sports Equipment, Clothes That Don't Fit and Tools I'll Never Use.

Entry to the Echo Bay Museum is by donation. Make it a good one—all proceeds go to the Scott Cove Hatchery for salmonid enhancement.

THE CORTES CASTLE
CORTES ISLAND

We've all heard that a man's home is his castle. When Karl Triller immigrated to Canada from Hungary in 1951, maybe no one told him that the phrase was only a figure of speech. He built a five-storey castle on Cortes Island, one of the Discovery Islands between the mainland and Campbell River.

Triller based the castle's design on the many ancient European castles he had dreamed of as a child and had visited before emigrating. Tranquil Cortes Island is an unlikely place to spot a castle. It lies at the entrance to Desolation Sound and is better known for its kayaking than its architecture. With fewer than 1000 residents on the island, King Karl's castle at the end of Manzanita Road stands out.

The castle's official name is Wolf Bluff, after the animals that roamed the area before Triller arrived. He says the wolves watched with curiosity for the 12 years it took to complete construction on his masterpiece. Cement blocks—13,000 of them in total—provide the castle's structure. Lugging the cement up to the top turret was a challenge for Triller, who did most of the work on his own and also built all the furniture in the house. He employed a pony to help drag logs up from the beach and improvised a simple pulley system to haul materials to the upper five storeys.

Two of the turrets facing Cortes Bay contain cannons, probably to fend off attacks from Discovery Island pirates, or nosy photographers.

Under the medieval-esque main floors hides a dungeon that would make Henry VIII proud. The air is dark and musty, and to accentuate the macabre atmosphere, Truller stuffed ragged clothes with fibreglass to stage elaborate torture scenes. I can't fathom why anyone would want to get married here—but lots of couples do. Triller, a former chef, used to cater the events, but now he just provides the venue.

As for the King of Cortes, he's been thinking of abdicating, if someone makes him a princely offer.

GOING YORKY
YORKE ISLAND

The British gained control of the coastal land that would later be called British Columbia after a drawn-out skirmish with Russia, France and Spain. In 1930, still feeling territorial, the Canadian Militia established a compound on Yorke Island during World War II, because it feared an attack from Japanese boats coming through Johnstone Strait. The attack never came, inspiring one writer to quip that the area is "better known for killer whales than killer subs."

Curious island hoppers can still explore parts of the crumbling barracks, as well as some meeting rooms and ammunition storage areas. Though the 260 men stationed on Yorke lived there for weeks or months at a time, I'd definitely make sure my boat's gas tank held enough fuel for a round trip before heading to the island. Too much time spent on Yorke Island might not be that good for one's mental health. The numerous reported cases of cabin fever led to a special term for the condition: Going Yorky.

BROTHER XII AND
THE AQUARIAN FOUNDATION
DECOURCY ISLAND

It's fitting that sharing the story of Brother XII and his failed Utopian cult poses certain risks to the teller. Some say that a curse extends to all who write about the Aquarian Foundation—a failed-utopian brotherhood that newspapers associated with black magic during its heyday and downfall. Kayakers, boaters and visitors to DeCourcy Island have long hunted for the legendary fortune amassed by Brother XII. According to rumours, gold coins stashed in glass jars then enclosed in cedar crates hide somewhere on DeCourcy. Islands made of limestone have lots of places to disguise treasure. In addition to the buildings and dugouts built by the foundation, the land itself has pockets, caves and fissures all over.

Brother XII, aka Edward Arthur Wilson, aka Julian Churton Skottowe, had long been fascinated by the occult and believed that he was a messenger with a direct link to the "Masters of Wisdom." He established a colony just south of Nanaimo, on Vancouver Island. There is little agreement about the man's origins. Some say he was born Edward Arthur Wilson in 1878 and served as a British sea captain. Other accounts place him as a teenager named Julian Churton Skottowe, son of a church missionary in Wyoming, Ontario. His origins don't really matter, though; the real trouble began when this false prophet arrived on Vancouver Island.

Followers began to arrive in the late 1920s, attracted by the promise of a connection to the Masters of Wisdom, who would help Brother XII create a universal brotherhood. Early disciples played on the beach and dug for clams at Cedar-by-the-Sea, just south of Nanaimo. Many of the early recruits were English astrologers such as Alfred and Annie Barley, as well as the infamous Madame Zee, who became Brother XII's lover and partner.

Originally named Mabel Rowbothan, she was notorious for her anger and sadism; rumours began to circulate that she liked to carry a horsewhip.

The Utopian community quickly started to receive bad press. Headlines such as "Cult Holds Members as Slaves on BC Island" and "Black Magic, Gold and Guns Feature Strange Cult Case" appeared around the province.

With the assistance of wealthy patron Mary Connally, the Aquarian Foundation purchased DeCourcy Island, 122 wild hectares next to Valdes Island, in 1928. The colony's three primary locations, at Cedar-by-the-Sea, DeCourcy Island and Valdes Island represented three distinct levels of discipleship according to Brother XII's teachings.

So just where did these teaching originate? Brother XII claimed to receive instructions from the "Masters of Wisdom," who directed all affairs of the Aquarian Foundation.

He predicted the end of the world's economic system, so the farm on DeCourcy Island was essential to his long-term plans of complete sustainability within the community. He called the island his "City of Refuge." Back at Cedar-by-the-Sea, the "House of Mystery" was the most important building constructed by the colony. The one-room cabin became the sanctuary of Brother XII when he retreated to meditate.

The colony fell apart in the early 1930s, as abuse in the Aquarian Foundation community became increasingly harsh. Followers were forced to work 24-hour shifts in the field. Brother XII grew increasingly paranoid about his safety and demanded numerous mini-forts be constructed for protection. DeCourcy Island's harbour made the government's attempts to investigate the island very dangerous. Brother XII armed a stone fort near the harbour with rifles, and he could flee to any of the other forts to avoid interrogation.

Followers had sacrificed all their money and possessions upon joining the foundation. When Brother XII disappeared with Madame Zee, some believe that the money, $20 gold coins totalling $400,000 by some estimates, stayed hidden in the multiple vaults on the island. None of this gold has been found, though treasure seekers still journey to DeCourcy Island to find the Aquarian Foundation fortune.

BIG
GARGANTUAN & RIDICULOUSLY OVERSIZED

World's Largest Wind Chimes

The world's biggest wind chimes beckon visitors to Figments, a mountain crafts store in Kaslo. Loudly. Built on the profits of timber claims, Kaslo has adapted to the times.

Since its incorporation in 1893, Kaslo's primary industry has transitioned from forestry to silver mining, railway building, fruit production and, finally, tourism. Through these changes, Kaslo has maintained a Victorian flair that echoes back to the rich expansion days of the British Empire. I had no idea the Victorians were so fond of wind chimes.

JAMES ISLAND

James Island is the chameleon of BC, able to transform and reinvent itself every few decades. The tiny island (only 315 hectares in total) is located beside Sidney Island, only a few kilometres off the east coast of Vancouver Island. James Island had humble beginnings. Farm families who settled there in the 1870s named the small piece of land after James Douglas, a former governor of Vancouver Island.

For 30 years, the farmers led a peaceful existence, but around 1900, the island suddenly became a private hunting ground for Victoria's wealthy elite. Some families were forced to leave and others left willingly after the sportsmen's invasion.

Thirteen years passed, and the progression of World War I was cause for another James Island transformation. Canadian Explosives Ltd. built a dynamite plant and imported 800 workers to live and work on the island. At its peak rate, before World War II, the plant produced 900 tonnes of TNT per month. That's a lot of explosives to be housed on a small island.

After its closure in 1962, the plant and village were disassembled. James Island looked like the pristine, uninhabited land it had been 100 years earlier. But not for long.

Today, James Island is once again a rich kid's playground. A Jack Nicklaus—designed golf course and six deluxe cottages encourage wealthy visitors. A seaplane ramp accommodates those who choose to fly in for a weekend and a commercial grade dock was built to harbour large yachts.

On the Road

Cue the Willie Nelson tunes, because it's time to buckle your seatbelt and head on a road trip over the highways, gravel roads and famous bridges of British Columbia.

From a taste of Olde England and unexpected road signs to the dirtiest park in Canada, this chapter visits all the places along the road where you'd want to pull over, get out a camera and take a second look.

LOTZKAR MEMORIAL PARK
GREENWOOD

Greenwood, Canada's smallest incorporated city, boomed during the mining years. Robert Wood arrived in the Boundary Creek Valley in 1895 and purchased, on a hunch, 81 hectares of land near the mouth of Deadwood Gulch for $5000. His vision of "Greenwood Camp," the name he gave to the store and a set of subdivided lots, was of a bustling city, central to the mass-producing mines and independent sites in the area.

In the early years of the 20th century, Greenwood boasted 17 hotels, numerous saloons and over 3000 residents. American companies built smelters, and the mines seemed inexhaustible. Open 24 hours per day, the mines produced record amounts of ore—in some years, 9 tonnes for every man employed. But by 1912, the inexhaustible mines were tired.

Aside from its mining history, Greenwood enjoyed a brief return to Canadian prominence at the beginning of the World War II. On February 2, 1942, the Ministry of National Defence decided all "enemy aliens"—the Japanese who lived in Canada—had to be removed from the West Coast. With only a couple hundred of citizens remaining, Greenwood could certainly make room for the diaspora of relocated Japanese. The Ohaira Gardens became the centre of Japanese culture in Greenwood—a work-hard, drink-hard mining town. The garden has since reverted to nature.

Today, the most noticeable thing about Greenwood as you drive into town is the huge slag pile and imposing smokestack. From the highway, the slag pile looks like a fluid black mass, a thick puddle about to slide down the side of the valley. The smelting waste took on the bell-shaped mould of the slag cars. These "Hell's Bells," as they came to be known, look like towering gravestones, or giant burned marshmallows. The waste slag glowed red in the night during the smelter's reign over Greenwood, but it now sits in black heaps. For some reason,

elementary schools in the area feel the need to take classes of
children up here. At least they did when I was in elementary
school. The area has been renamed Lotzkar Memorial Park—
it has the distinction of being Canada's dirtiest park.

World's Biggest Tree Crusher

The world's tallest living tree, the Stratosphere Giant, measuring almost 113 metres high, is in the Rockefeller Forest of the Humboldt Redwoods State Park in California, not Mackenzie.

The world's tallest-ever tree was a eucalyptus, reported in 1872. Forester William Ferguson measured the tree at 132.6 metres tall, near Watts River in Victoria, Australia, not Mackenzie.

The world's fattest tree is the European chestnut, also known as the "tree of 100 horses," presumably because it would take that many horses to dislodge it. Before it split into three pieces, the tree had a circumference of almost 58 metres when it was measured in 1780 on Mount Etna, in Sicily, Italy, not Mackenzie.

The world's largest forest is the vast coniferous forest in northern Russia. The forest covers 1.1 billion hectares near the Arctic Circle, not Mackenzie.

And yet Mackenzie has the world's largest tree crusher. It was brought to Mackenzie to clear the trees from a valley that flooded when the dam was built. In a minimum amount of time and at low cost, the 17-metre-long steel crusher allowed one machine and one operator to do the work of many. The same couldn't be said of the time and expense involved to get it to Mackenzie. It took six flatbed railway cars to transport the powerful machine to Mackenzie and four days to assemble it, once there. Transporting the crusher to the work site took another three weeks at the end of 1964, all to go a distance of approximately 7 kilometres. The crusher got stuck several times, its rollers iced up and the grade of a hill had to be cut to allow the giant to climb it; all transit activity ceased for that year!

The situation didn't improve much once the machine reached the work site. The crusher broke down constantly and got stuck. Finally, in the summer of 1965, luck changed and the crusher covered 910.5 hectares in a matter of months.

By 1984, the crusher, which hadn't seen action in several years, had become an eyesore at Out Thumb Creek. No one wanted it left in its present location, but the thought of moving it was nearly as distasteful. A committee formed, and soon, BC Forest Products Ltd. stepped in to help. The crusher, disassembled once again, was moved to Mackenzie Boulevard in the downtown core on October 19, 1984.

Many locals turned up on moving day to snap pictures of the eyesore, which is now marketed as a site-to-see for tourist. It's the attraction that locals love to hate.

THE NELSON MURALS
NELSON

Since the arrival of many hippies and draft dodgers of the Vietnam War in the 1960s and 1970s, the towns and cities situated off the beaten track in southeastern BC have attracted the "art scene." Writers, filmmakers and artists live in the region, and Nelson, with its dramatic snow-capped mountains, still lakes and arts college, has become a hub. John Villani named Nelson one of Canada's leading arts towns.

Downtown, at the south end of Vernon street, four murals painted by high school art students loom over the streets. The murals depict historic scenes: the K&S Railroad at Payne Bluffs, one of the first major mines in the area; *Nasookin,* the famous stern wheeler, trapped in the ice; Nelson's streetcar number 3; and the giant nose of Steve Martin.

What?

There's no mistake. The fourth "historic" mural in downtown Nelson features comedian Steve Martin in a scene from *Roxanne,* wearing a giant, pointed, Pinocchio-style schnoz. The romantic comedy was filmed in Nelson in 1986, drawing loads of tourists and dollars to the area. The city of Nelson must have been grateful to Martin for selecting the city, but wouldn't a thank-you card have sufficed?

BEACON HILL PARK
VICTORIA

With its playgrounds, duck ponds and classical music performances each Sunday, Beacon Hill Park, near downtown Victoria, is a popular weekend spot for families. Parents heading for the adventure playground with misbehaving kids have threatened to lock them in the monkey cages and pick them up later. At least, mine did.

These threats never get taken all that seriously. The monkey cages don't look convincing; the circular concrete structures look more suited to storing park maintenance equipment than animals. Today, the only exotic animals that call Beacon Hill Park home are the moody peacocks that live near the petting zoo.

Beacon Hill Park attracted visitors as a zoo back in 1889, with a motley crew of six deer, a bear, sheep, an eagle, two swans and pheasants. The zoo didn't purchase animals or birds according to a plan, though the *Colonist* reported in 1901 that the zoo hoped to get "a cage of monkeys and a pair of foxes" from the zoo in Vancouver. Donated animals frequently arrived for free and often turned up unexpectedly.

Likely, the park staff was untrained in how to care for these animals, and more likely, it was strapped for places to house them. Staff hastily constructed quarters from whatever materials could be found on short notice. The result was miserable conditions and inadequate care for the animals, much like European zoos of the 19th century.

The conditions at Beacon Hill certainly weren't "funny" weird, but they were definitely bizarre. The buildings for the tropical plants were the height of greenhouse technology at the time, with lots of light and shelter. The animals lived in dark wet pits and were fed meals composed primarily of bread and milk with boiled rice.

Zoo conditions did not improve much in the 20th century. Reports from the 1930s to the 1960s have been labelled by David Hancocks, a zoo historian, as the "disinfectant years." The so-called modern cages opposed everything in the animals' natural environment. They were clinically sterile with smooth concrete floors and nothing more than a stainless steel pole for entertainment.

After these grim years, no more large animals came to Beacon Hill Park. In 1973, the Children's Petting Zoo, maintained by Park employees, opened near the deer enclosure. Today, the petting zoo is run privately and remains open seasonally for the animals' well being. A sad memory for the genteel city of Victoria.

BIG GARGANTUAN & RIDICULOUSLY OVERSIZED

World's Tallest Totem Pole

The totem poles of the Pacific Northwest may be the most recognizable signs of First Nations' culture in the region. A totem is defined as an object, such as a plant or animal, that symbolically represents a person or kinship group. The First Nations cultures carved these emblems into wooden poles that were displayed. Every animal carved into the pole represents a creature whose spiritual powers are associated with the family, and the stylized faces represent the ancestry of an individual. Designs were traditionally drawn in charcoal, carved, then painted with a mixture of minerals combined with salmon eggs.

Carvers created different types of poles for many reasons. Among the Kwakwaka'wakw and Nuu-chah-nulth, a tall, slender pole with a bird figure perched on top customarily adorned the house of a chief. In some Haida villages, many homes had portal poles built into the front of the house, with an oval doorway carved into the pole to be used as an entrance for

☞

BIG **GARGANTUAN &** **RIDICULOUSLY** **OVERSIZED** special ceremonies. In downtown Victoria, the "totems" created by (what are presumed to be) naughty teens are considered vandalism of the city's telephone poles.

The title "World's Largest Totem Pole" has been claimed by several towns and cities, and, not surprisingly, three of the five totems can be found in British Columbia—in Vancouver, Victoria and Alert Bay. The Alert Bay totem towers over the others with a height of 56.4 metres, but disputes over construction (Alert Bay's totem is crafted from two pieces of wood) or local affiliations of the carver have arisen. However, the two pieces of wood used in the Alert Bay totem pole measure 55 metres and 1.4 metres tall, and the next tallest totem, in Kalama, Washington, measures much less. The Alert Bay totem pole features 22 figures and stretches so high that it requires binoculars to make out the details at the top.

The thickest totem pole, carved in 1988 by Richard Hunt, measures 1.8 metres in diameter and can be found in Duncan, the "Totem Capital."

BE PREPARED FOR THE UNEXPECTED

PORT HARDY

With 97 percent of Vancouver Island's population living on the island's south end, those seeking solitude and outdoor adventure come north to Port Hardy—the northernmost point on the Island Highway. Named after Vice-Admiral Sir Thomas Masterman Hardy, Port Hardy provides ferry service to the Queen Charlotte Islands and Prince Rupert. Logging has long been an important industry to the area, but much of the land is protected. Cape Scott provincial park provides wild hiking trails that are not for the inexperienced; sharp climbs, muddy trails, frosty evenings and direct sun exposure are all part of a day's hike. The prize for withstanding Mother Nature in the raw? Tranquility untouched by commercial industry.

In addition to the outdoor recreation, those who travel this far north on Vancouver Island are treated to one of the funniest road signs in Canada. West of Port Hardy, a gravel road leads towards Holberg, past clear blue lakes and deep forests. The roads can be dangerous, especially in winter. Tight corners, windstorms and old trees sometimes make for a nasty combination. "Always be prepared for the unexpected" is the motto for the road, expressed by a large yellow sign. The yellow sign is like any other in the province, except that instead of perching atop a metal bar, the sign rests against an enormous felled tree... that's resting atop a totalled white car. The car appears to have been crawling out of a sand pile when the tree fell on it. OK, maybe that's not how it happened, but who knows? Travellers along the road have been known to place stuffed animals in a hole in the centre of the tree's trunk.

GRAVITY HILL
ABBOTSFORD, BC

I'd often heard stories of a place in Abbotsford where your car, out of gear with its brakes off, would be pulled uphill, as if by some magical force. Abbotsford, a meeting of urban and rural lifestyles in the Fraser Valley, is dedicated to its farming history, yet it embraces its city life, too. Visitors can spend the day on an in-depth farm tour or hiking and fishing, and then come back to town for a night of fine dining, classical music and theatre.

Gravity Hill is not listed on the city's website as an attraction to see, and only avid golfers would come across it by chance. The hill can be found on McKee Road, near the Ledgeview golf course.

This attraction can be enjoyed on the most modest of travel budgets. All that's needed is a car to get there, or, if you're walking, a pop can to roll down (up!) the road. Some people might call this littering, but here in weird BC, we call it tourism. If it doesn't take much to amuse you, Gravity Hill should definitely make its way onto your to-do list of things to experience.

Gravity hills are more common than you might think, with many found in the U.S. and Canada. New Brunswick's Magnetic Hill is another famous one. Usually, these hills can be found where the level horizon is obscured—often by other hills. Because of the other hills, visual clues such as trees or buildings lean slightly, creating an optical illusion that makes a slight downhill look like an uphill. Whether the illusion gets blamed on faulty gravity or strong magnetism in the area, locals usually market the sites as tourist attractions. The places are often ascribed mysterious powers or mythical stories to explain the irregularity. Science, of course, proves that it's our eyes that are faulty, not the earth.

BIG
GARGANTUAN &
RIDICULOUSLY
OVERSIZED

World's Tallest Tin Soldier

Soldiers of the Royal Engineers founded New Westminster in 1864. In their honour, and as a monument to celebrate the Festival of Trees, Austin Metal Fabricators in Burnaby constructed the world's tallest tin soldier. He stands 9.8 metres tall and was actually constructed of stainless steel, not tin. Artifacts from the year 2000 and earlier rest inside the soldier's massive body, to be opened in 2025.

CAMELSFOOT RANGE
THE CARIBOO

The Camelsfoot Range, a subrange of the Chilcotin Range in the Coast Mountains, commemorates the strange role these desert animals played during the gold rush. In a contest of strange entrepreneurial ideas, this one may qualify as the weirdest in Canadian history because of its huge initial cost and just how overwhelmingly bad the experiment turned out for everyone involved.

During the Cariboo gold rush years, freight competition was stiff. Packers who ran raw materials and goods between the many camps and cities needed to offer the best prices, or the most competent horses and mules, to prosper at the challenging and dangerous work. Frank Laumeister, a prominent Victoria merchant and packer, chose to think outside the box—outside the continent, really—to give his packing business an edge. How could he move more goods, faster, and with less cost than anyone else? Frank decided to employ the "ship of the desert" to help move huge amounts of cargo to the remote interior outposts. These desert ships, two-hump camels, could out-walk and out-carry any animal known in North America. The camels could apparently go six to ten days without water, travel up to 70 kilometres daily and carry loads weighing 500 kilograms.

A load of camels had arrived in Arizona months earlier; presumably, an American packer had similar notions for their use. Twenty-three of the Bactrian camels travelled to San Francisco, where they were then loaded on a steamer, the *Enterprise*, to head for Canada. Laumeister paid $6000 for the camels, a hefty sum in those days. When the camels arrived in the Caribou in May of 1862, they packed along the Fraser River Canyon.

Other packers were surely peeved over the loss of business they were doomed to suffer, but they had a more immediate reason to be angry. Horses from competing freight outfitters would stampede at the sight of a camel, creating extensive losses. A story in Victoria's local daily on May 29, 1862, reported the journal comments of Clement Cornwall, presumably a freight outfitter: "Met two camels on the road...The horses were tremendously frightened." The camels bit and kicked everything and smelled so rank that other animals would take off, load and all. Sometimes, in their haste to escape the stinky camels, horses and mules would fall off the roads to their deaths.

The situation wasn't wonderful for Laumeister, either. The camels successfully travelled for many hours without resting and maintained their diet from the grasses and sages along the Cariboo Wagon Road. But, after acclimating to the area, the camels began to experiment with other, more convenient foods. They would eat anything from a pair of pants to a bar of soap and were constantly ill because of something they'd swallowed. Laumeister couldn't trust them not to devour the goods upon their backs.

The biggest hindrance to turning a profit was the loss of camels. Though sturdy and surefooted on a sandy desert, the camels had less confidence on the steep rocky canyons of the Cariboo. The soles of their feet were easy torn by the rough terrain, so Laumeister had to outfit the troop with little booties made of canvas and rawhide. In addition, the camels never proved able to handle loads exceeding 300 kilograms. One unfortunate camel was mistaken for a grizzly bear by miner John Morris in Quesnel Forks. After blasting the beast, Morris and his companions were surprised to find that their grizzly was a camel, now with a hole in its side. Within four months of the camels' Cariboo introduction, the government outlawed the use of camels on the trail.

Laumeister sold his remaining camels to ranchers throughout BC; many escaped into the wilds of the Camelsfoot mountain range. No one knows how much of Laumeister's initial investment was returned to him, but it's seems obvious that he had to chalk up the whole experiment as a learning experience. The last camel of the original 23 died in Ashcroft in 1905, or in 1910 by some records. Despite its death, sightings of lone camels continued; into the late 1930s, farmers in the region complained of camels destroying their gardens. Even today, the odd rancher (or, more likely, tourist, tired of the endless rock faces and trees on the drive through the Cariboo) "spots" a camel silhouetted in the woods. As camels are ungulates, some have wondered about the possibility of camels cross-breeding with moose or deer, but these stories carry even less weight than Sasquatch or Ogopogo sightings do. If you're driving through the region though, keep your eyes (and noses) alert for any humped-back moose or deer with sore feet.

HOLBERG SHOE TREE
HOLBERG

In the early years of the twentieth century, Danish colonists moved to northern Vancouver Island and named a settlement after Baron Ludwig Holberg, a historian and playwright. About a 90-minute drive west from Port Hardy, the land surrounding Holberg boasts the best of the coastal rainforest: enormous trees, lush plant life, white sand beaches and diverse wildlife.

Once the home of the world's largest floating logging camp, Holberg is completely land-based today. Travellers come from around the globe to partake in world-class fishing, scenic kayak trips or to hike the challenging Cape Scott Trail.

The Cape Scott Trail traces an old telegraph line through old-growth Sitka spruce and cedar. Hikers nearing the end of the trail will encounter an odd beacon of homecoming as they return to Holberg: a shoe tree laden with hundreds of worn-down shoes retired after the long (17 hour) hike.

The strangest element of the shoe tree is not its existence, but the range of shoes hanging from it. Boots, sandals and even strappy high heels have been attached to the old cedar snag. My question isn't, "Why?" but "*Who* wears high heels in the middle of the woods in Holberg?"

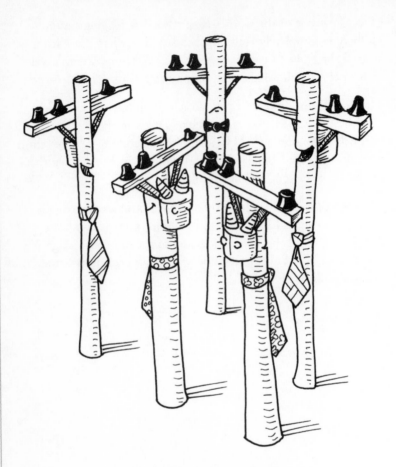

ALL DRESSED UP,
BUT NO PLACE TO GO
AINSWORTH HOT SPRINGS

The tiny village of Ainsworth Hot Springs can be found nestled in the centre of the Kootenay Wilderness, between Balfour and Kaslo. The heart of the village is, what a surprise, the mineral hot springs, which forms in a dark horseshoe-shaped cave just north of Kootenay Lake.

People travelling to the hot springs will notice something strange as they head north on Highway 31: a number of the telephone poles appear to be wrapped in streamers. After closer inspection, it becomes clear that the bright stripes aren't streamers but a succession of men's neckties.

Why the ties were hung and who did it remains a local mystery. Some people say that John Lennon fans hung them in tribute to his last album, which had ties on the cover. Others believe that groups of back-to-the-land types who escaped from the city hung their ties up as they arrived in the rural area. The best story claims that the ties were purchased from the BC Hydro Ugly Tie Auction, an event that no longer takes place. The man who bought them hung the ties as markers to direct friends to his retirement celebration, sort of like balloons at children's birthday parties. No matter which version is the truth, the tradition carries on. In the 1980s the ties carried on for several kilometres, starting from Toad Rock. The original ties have long since been stripped from the poles because of the weather, but every few years in June, high school grad students steal Dad's ugliest tie and decorate the highway.

If hot springs and ugly ties aren't enough to draw you to Ainsworth, the neighbouring town of Balfour offers the world's longest free ferry ride—a 40-minute crossing of Kootenay Lake.

WEIRD WOODS

REVELSTOKE

Peter Watts operated his property on the south side of Highway 1 as a tourist attraction known as "Weird Woods." Just what was so weird about the woods is unclear. Watts passed away in 1994 at the age of 57, and all that remains of his attraction today is the enormous statue of Smokey the Bear. Watts built the 9-metre-tall bear by hand in 1967; maybe he intended for Smokey to watch over the woods for eternity.

Today, the Smokey Bear Campground stands where "Weird Woods" once delighted visitors (with something weird, I hope.) The woods live on at least in name; maps with directions to the world's largest Smokey Bear still read: "Weird Woods Road."

World's Largest Cuckoo Clock

Situated between the Rockies and the Purcell Mountains, Kimberley likens itself to a European city, or more specifically, the "Bavarian City of the Rockies." In the 1970s, someone decided that BC needed a little more Bavaria. Kimberley answered the challenge, though the city has deeper roots to South Africa than Europe. Miners named Kimberley after the South African diamond mine of the same name, in the hope that the BC city's mineral reserves would be as profitable. Nevertheless, the downtown centre, known affectionately as the Platzl, is adorned with colourful hanging baskets in summer, highlighting the European architecture and design of the storefronts. Kimberley is home to the "Old Bauernhaus" building, originally built in southern Bavaria about 350 years ago. In 1987, it was taken apart and shipped to Kimberley, where the reconstructed building now houses the ☞

BIG GARGANTUAN & RIDICULOUSLY OVERSIZED Bauernhaus Restaurant. Kimberley also hosts the "greatest accordion show on the planet" each summer at the International Olde Time Accordion Championships.

The most obvious example of Kimberley's European spirit can be found right downtown at the Platzl pedestrian mall. Not a restaurant…not an accordion store…but the world's biggest cuckoo clock. The nearly 7-metre-high clock can be read from far down the street, but even visitors "hard of sight" will know the time. Happy Hans, the town mascot emerges every hour and yodels. Visitors who can't wait for the top of the hour can insert a quarter, and Hans will yodel on request.

CAPILANO SUSPENSION BRIDGE
VANCOUVER

Few British Columbians have the opportunity to go to a real circus with sequined acrobats walking a tightrope high above their heads. At least not in their home province. Many BC-ers, on the other hand, can go to Capilano Suspension Bridge and feel like tightrope walkers themselves, sequins optional.

In 1888, George Grant Mackay, a Scottish civil engineer and land developer, immigrated to the young and bustling city of Vancouver, which had only been incorporated two years earlier and had a population of under 15,000 people. Mackay purchased 2428 hectares of thickly wooded land surrounding the Capilano River and built a small wood cabin on the very edge of the canyon wall. With the help of horses and First Nations People who lived nearby, he constructed a thin, shaky bridge of hemp and cedar planks. The First Nations nicknamed the rustic construction the "laughing bridge" because of the sound it made when the wind blew. But crossing the bridge was no laughing matter; only the most adventurous of Mackay's friends ventured across it or made the long trek through the forest to even reach his cabin. The bridge stretched 137 metres long over the jagged rocks and rushing waters 70 metres below.

After Mackay's death, the hemp and cedar bridge was replaced with a wire cable bridge. A new opportunity arose; crossing the bridge still brought the same rush of adrenalin and accomplishment, but it was now completely safe. Vancouver's first tourist trap was born.

Today, the 11-hectare park that encloses the Capilano Suspension Bridge includes Tree-Top Adventure—a series of seven smaller suspension bridges that string 30 metres above ground along the evergreens guided nature walks, the Living Forest, First Nations carving exhibits and first-class meals served on a patio.

Locals know a secret about the Capilano Suspension Bridge. Concerts during the Vancouver Jazz Fest in June and July take place on the grounds. Any other time, for the pleasure of crossing the bridge, visitors can expect to hand over a hefty sum (in 2006, it would set you back $25.95). During Jazz Fest? Free.

A YARD ONLY A MOTHER COULD LOVE

SALMON ARM

At first glance, Bert and Gladys Stewart's house in Salmon Arm looks like the aftermath of a toddler's birthday party: ceramic animals, pink flamingos and plastic toys roam the lawn, along with garden gnomes, wooden cartoon characters and a tiny Jersey cow, just chillin' out in the sun.

Bert and Gladys don't host children's birthday parties, though; nor are they messy or forgetful about where they leave their possessions. This seeming mess is intentional—it's a home for unwanted lawn ornaments.

When people move, they drop their extra "stuff" at the Stewarts, knowing it will find a home on their large front lawn. The occasional nighttime visitor makes a silent donation to the collection, too. Not all the ornaments are cast offs; Bert builds his own windmills and whirligigs, hangs plastic fruit in the live trees on the property and stacks bedpans near the front door.

So, what does one do with a lawn-full of ornaments? Why, show it off! Over the years, Bert and Gladys have welcomed curious guests from around the globe to their home in the northern Okanagan. In addition, buses of visitors from local hospitals drop by during summer, usually once or twice every week.

The most frequent question the Stewarts deal with: how do you mow the lawn?

BIG
GARGANTUAN &
RIDICULOUSLY
OVERSIZED

Catch of the Day

With the Pacific to the west, anglers hoping to land the "big one" might look past the interior of the province for great fishing. What a shame. Within BC, the best-known fish may be the famous Kamloops trout, the Gerrard—the world's largest breed of rainbow trout. It can only be found in Kootenay Lake.

In 1993, Kamloops celebrated its centennial and also hosted the World Fly-Fishing Championships. In honour of both events, the Kamloops Wood Carvers (Ed Ferner, Vern Smith, Bruce Hulbert, Art Tremblay, Dave Rolston, Gerry Watson and Willy Wilkinson) carved a 4.5-metre-long trout out of cedar that weighed in at 565 kilograms. By far, it's the biggest catch this town's ever seen. The huge trout perches on top of an upside-down metal cone. It appears to have been speared mid-swim by one of those pointy paper cups you sip from at the dentist's office.

A LITTLE BIT OF OLDE ENGLAND
VICTORIA

Where in Canada can you visit Queen Victoria, Queen Elizabeth, Princess Diana, three Princes of Wales, the Duke and Duchess of Windsor, a beheaded Anne Boleyn, Margaret Thatcher and Winston Churchill (all before lunch), and then go for high tea in a royal setting? Only in Victoria—the city that's more British than Britain herself.

The downtown core of Victoria offers every delight for the British soul: high tea is served with savouries and dainties at the massive Fairmont Empress Hotel or at the Blethering Place; British Sweet shops line Government Street, stretching from the inner harbour into town; and the Royal London Wax Museum, a somewhat musty little building, takes visitors back in time and across the Atlantic. The staff even dress in period costume.

The World of Wax originally opened in 1961 on the street level of the Crystal Gardens in downtown Victoria. With approximately 90 figures, it became the first venue in North America showing the work of Josephine Tussaud—proprietor of the famous Madame Tussaud's in England.

Though some modern celebrities, cartoon characters and sports heroes made the cut, the Royal London Wax Museum delights in showcasing primarily historical British figures and torture scenes. Great for the whole family! Special exhibits include the Crown Jewels Theatre, the World War I Field Surgical Hospital Kit and the original opera chairs crafted for the Prince and Princess of Wales in 1987.

The shops on Government Street have been modernized over the years, and the Empress Hotel continues to change hands, becoming a little more North Americanized with each transaction. The Royal London Wax Museum remains a stronghold for the little corner of Olde England that still exists in Victoria today.

A NOT-SO-HEARTY WELCOME
COALMONT

A few hours east of Vancouver, along the Crowsnest Highway, lies the city of Princeton, better known as the last chance for gas before Manning Park if you're driving west. When driving east, people like to joke that Princeton is beyond hope, meaning Hope, BC. And if that's the case, Coalmont is even further beyond hope. Some know Coalmont as "the little town that never quite made it."

As suggested by the name, Coalmont got its start as a coal-mining town. In the 1850s, a prospector discovered an outcropping of coal along the Similkameen River. The vein lay fully exposed; you could have set it alight with a match. The miners were amazed that a bolt of lightening hadn't done the deed already. The Canadian Pacific Railway became a major customer for Coalmont, because the new railways needed tonnes of coal to power their steam engines. For decades, Coalmont prospered as a mining town; houses, general stores, bars and hotels, including the famous Coalmont Hotel, covered the dry, grassy fields. By the 1920s, problems arose at the mine. The coal supply wasn't an issue, but the quality posed a threat: workers could die if the stockpiled coal spontaneously combusted. Mine owners regarded the danger as a token possibility. Who cares about spontaneous combustion when the money's rolling in? On August 13, 1930, the inevitable token explosion killed 48 miners. They were all buried in the town cemetery.

Today, travelling bikers sit most frequently on the stools at the Old Coalmont Hotel bar. Visitors aren't welcomed with much enthusiasm. If you turn off Highway 3 onto Tulameen Road, you'll pull right into the village centre. Beside the dusty gravel road, on sparse yellowed grass, stand two "welcome" signs to the village of Coalmont. The first reads:

> *You are approaching the peaceful little village of Coalmont.*
> *Population: Varies. Industry: None. Chief Sports: Sleeping and*
> *Day Dreaming. Climate: Hot—cold—wet—dry—at various*
> *times. All clubs and lodges hold their meetings at midnight on*
> *the sixth Tuesday of each month. Coalmont welcomes you and*
> *will be delighted to serve you—provided you are lucky enough*
> *to find us open.*

The second sign makes no pretence of welcome. At the top of the sign, someone has painted a giant skull, like the ones found on poisonous oven cleaner. The sign serves due notice:

> *WARNING: To all doorstep salesmen—especially those selling*
> *magazines, encyclopedias and fire bells—your safe passage is not*
> *guaranteed in this village. Women beware! There is a predomi-*
> *nance of bachelors living here.*

I'd make a U-turn and not look back.

ABOUT THE AUTHOR

Michelle Simms

Michelle Simms lives in Victoria, BC. She has also lived in South Africa and Toronto but returned to her home province in 2002 to pursue creative writing at the University of Victoria. Her interest in BC stories and places grew from conversations with the regulars in a downtown Victoria espresso bar. Since then, learning and writing about the province has been one of her passions. When she's battling writer's block, Michelle puts on her inspirational pink hat that is decorated with buttons, fortune cookie messages and one bunny ear. Her work has appeared in the *Peninsula News*. She wrote and edited for a centennial book on the Saanich area, *One Hundred Years, One Hundred Stories*.

ABOUT THE ILLUSTRATORS

Graham Johnson

Graham Johnson is an Edmonton-based illustrator and graphic designer. When he isn't drawing or designing, he...well...he's always drawing or designing! On the off-chance you catch him not doing one of those things, he's probably cooking, playing tennis or poring over other illustrations.

Roger Garcia

Roger Garcia immigrated to Canada from El Salvador at the age of seven. Because of the language barrier, he had to find a way to communicate with other kids. That's when he discovered the art of tracing. It wasn't long before he mastered this highly skilled technique, and by age 14, he was drawing weekly cartoons for the *Edmonton Examiner*. He taught himself to paint and sculpt; then in high school and college, Roger skipped class to hide in the art room all day in order to further explore his talent. Currently, Roger's work can be seen in a local weekly newspaper and in places around Edmonton.

BLUE BIKE BOOKS

NOW ENJOY THESE FUN- AND FACT-FILLED BOOKS OF BRITISH COLUMBIA AND CANADIAN TRIVIA...

Bathroom Book of British Columbia Trivia

British Columbians—last to vote in federal elections, first in earthquakes. Discover the oddities of beautiful BC, among them Fan Tan Alley, the narrowest street in North America.

$9.95 • ISBN10: 1-897278-02-0 • ISBN13: 978-1-897278-02-4 • 5.25" X 8.25" • 168 pages

Bathroom Book of British Columbia History

Given the mystique and unique landscape of British Columbia, why should its history be any different? In this eclectic collection of historic notables, you'll discover thousands of fascinating bits and pieces of BC's past. For example, the province once had its own navy; one notable premier changed his name, put shoe polish in his beard and was eventually declared insane; and BC was also the site of Canada's only Wild West shoot-out.

$9.95 • ISBN10: 1-897278-15-2 • ISBN13: 978-1-897278-15-4 • 5.25" X 8.25" • 168 pages

Bathroom Book of Canadian Trivia

An entertaining and lighthearted collection of illustrated factoids from across the country. You'll find beasties from the elusive lake monster Ogopogo to Canada's national emblem, the beaver—and you'll find culture and crime, such as the Calgary Stampede or the number of cars stolen in Canada and where they were stolen. This book has a myriad of informative tidbits to satisfy your curiosity and tickle your funny bone.

$9.95 • ISBN10: 0-9739116-0-3 • ISBN13: 978-0-9739116-0-2 • 5.25" X 8.25" • 144 pages

Bathroom Book of Canadian History

From wild weather to odd prime ministers, Canada's amazing history is full of the comic, the tragic and the just plain weird. You'll enjoy this fun collection of fascinating facts about our illustrious and often peculiar past.

$9.95 • ISBN10: 0-9739116-1-1 • ISBN13: 978-0-9739116-1-9 • 5.25" X 8.25" • 144 pages

Weird Canadian Places

The Canadian landscape is home to some pretty odd sights; for example, the UFO landing pad in St. Paul, Alberta, the ice hotel in Québec City or Casa Loma, Canada's only castle. This book humorously inventories many real estate oddities found across the country. Welcome to the True North—strange to see.

$9.95 • ISBN10: 0-9739116-4-6 • ISBN13: 978-0-9739116-4-0 • 5.25" X 8.25" • 168 pages

Available from your local bookseller or by contacting the distributor,
Lone Pine Publishing, at 1-800-661-9017.

www.lonepinepublishing.com